Norse Magic for Beginners

The Ultimate Guide to Norse Divination, Reading Elder Futhark Runes, and Spells

© Copyright 2021

The content within this book may not be reproduced, duplicated or transmitted without direct written permission from the author or the publisher.

Under no circumstances will any blame or legal responsibility be held against the publisher, or author, for any damages, reparation, or monetary loss due to the information within this book, either directly or indirectly.

Legal Notice:

This book is copyright protected. It is only for personal use. You cannot amend, distribute, sell, use, quote or paraphrase any part, or the content within this book, without the consent of the author or publisher.

Disclaimer Notice:

Please note the information within this document is for educational and entertainment purposes only. All effort has been executed to present accurate, up to date, reliable, complete information. No warranties of any kind are declared or implied. Readers acknowledge that the author is not engaging in the rendering of legal, financial, medical or professional advice. The content within this book has been derived from various sources. Please consult a licensed professional before attempting any techniques outlined in this book.

By reading this document, the reader agrees that under no circumstances is the author responsible for any losses, direct or indirect, that are incurred because of the use of information within this document, including, but not limited to, errors, omissions, or inaccuracies.

Your Free Gift (only available for a limited time)

Thanks for getting this book! If you want to learn more about various spirituality topics, then join Mari Silva's community and get a free guided meditation MP3 for awakening your third eye. This guided meditation mp3 is designed to open and strengthen ones third eye so you can experience a higher state of consciousness. Simply visit the link below the image to get started.

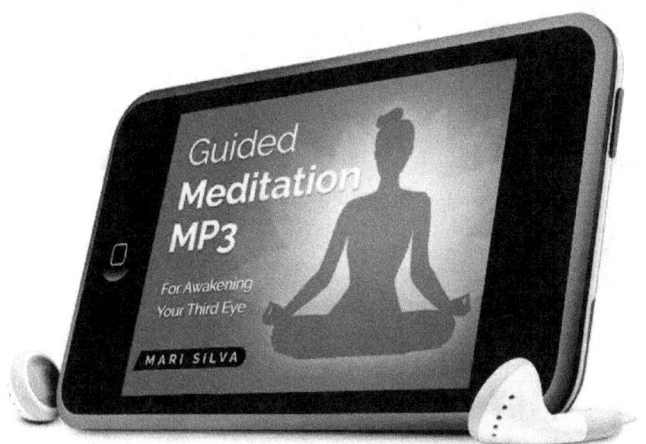

https://spiritualityspot.com/meditation

Contents

INTRODUCTION 1
CHAPTER 1: FOLLOWING THE FOOTSTEPS OF THE VIKINGS 3
    THE CREATION OF THE WORLD 4
    THE PANTHEON OF NORSE GODS 4
    RELIGIOUS PRACTICES 6
    MODERN GERMANIC/NORSE RELIGION AND PRACTICES 7
    WHAT IS ASATRO? 8
    PRACTICES OF HEATHENRY 10
    MORALITY AND ETHICS 11
    MAGIC AND SEERSHIP 12
CHAPTER 2: THE DIVINE GIFT OF FUTHARK 13
    THE ELDER FUTHARK 13
    MYTHICAL ORIGIN OF THE RUNES 14
    THE CONNECTION BETWEEN WOOD AND THE RUNES 16
    FUTHARK IN BRITAIN 17
    MODERN BELIEVERS 17
    WHAT CAN RUNES BE USED FOR? 18
    OTHER USES FOR RUNES 20
CHAPTER 3: THE FUNDAMENTALS OF DIVINATION 23
    THE IMPORTANCE OF MEDITATING BEFORE RUNE CASTING 25
    HOW MEDITATION CAN HELP WITH READINGS 26

- Preparing for Rune Casting 27
- A Quick Overview of the Casting Procedure 29
- How to Pick the Runes from the Casting Cloth 31

CHAPTER 4: THE RUNEMASTER'S TOOLS 32
- Making Your Own Runes 32
- Buying Commercially Available Runes 33
- Inscribing the Runes 38

CHAPTER 5: RUNE PREPARATION: FROM CLEANSING TO EMPOWERING 40
- The Proper Way to Store Your Runes 42
- Empowering Yourself 43

CHAPTER 6: AETTIR: THE MOTHER, THE WARRIOR, AND THE KING 46
- The Three Divisions 47
- Contradictions in Runes 49
- What to Expect from the Three Aettir? 49

CHAPTER 7: FREYA'S AETT 51

CHAPTER 8: HEIMDALL'S AETT 61

CHAPTER 9: TYR'S AETT 69
- Memorizing the Futhark Runes 78

CHAPTER 10: ODIN'S RUNE 83

CHAPTER 11: READING THE RUNES 90
- Rune Casting Layouts 91

CHAPTER 12: THE POEM OF THE GODS 106

CONCLUSION 118

HERE'S ANOTHER BOOK BY MARI SILVA THAT YOU MIGHT LIKE 119

YOUR FREE GIFT (ONLY AVAILABLE FOR A LIMITED TIME) 120

REFERENCES 121

Introduction

Do you love mythology? One topic you may find interesting is Norse mythology, particularly their ancient beliefs and the magical practices used in Norse witchcraft. If you have a strong interest in learning this magic, remember that you first need a solid foundation of the Nordic principles and beliefs. You have to build your knowledge about such tenets and beliefs to apply them when practicing Norse magic.

Few other cultures can compare with the intricacies and mystery surrounding the Norse. Their mythology is so vast and yet vague simultaneously. It is this unknown factor - the mystery - that makes people want to learn more about it. Of all the subjects covered about the ancient Norsemen, their divination and magical practices are among the most interesting.

Most people first learned about the ancient Norse through the mythologies surrounding the Asgardian gods they used to worship. It is all thanks to them getting the mainstream treatment in television, movies, comic books, and video games, but Norse magic involves more than just that.

It is where you will find this book, Norse Magic for Beginners: The Ultimate Guide to Norse Divination, Reading Elder Futhark Runes, and Spells, useful. This book will serve as your ultimate source of information regarding Norse magic. If you are a beginner, this book is what you have been looking for. It is easy to understand and contains updated information about Norse mythology and magic.

Even complex terms are explained simply, so those who have no idea what Norse is can easily grasp its meaning. This book will teach you about the supernatural practices that the ancient Norse people used to practice, like divination, rune casting, and how to cast an assortment of spells. This book is written so the whole learning process will become more fun and exciting.

I hope this book will quell your curiosity toward the Norse and their mysterious religious practices. I hope it will also inspire you to further your research about the Norse people and their colorful history.

Chapter 1: Following the Footsteps of the Vikings

Every time you hear the word "Norse," the Vikings may the first people that will most likely come to mind. Before the European colonizers forced them into Christianity, the Vikings and other Scandinavian tribes had their own pagan culture and religion. Thankfully, some ancient texts and practices survived the purge of the colonizers, and people are rediscovering them today.

The Norse, also called the Germanic religion, is polytheistic. It means that the people believed in many gods and goddesses - with each having different areas of expertise. There are gods/goddesses of love, agriculture, war, and many other aspects. Back then, who you worshipped would largely depend on your vocation or the community where you belonged.

The Creation of the World

According to the Norse (Old Germanic) pagan beliefs, the gods and all the beings who are in the Nine Worlds originated from a singular being, which is the giant known as Ymir, otherwise called Aurgelmir, Brimir, or Blainn. Legends say that Ymir was born from the water droplet that formed when the ice from Niflheim met the heat from Muspelheim.

Thanks to his hermaphroditic body, Ymir birthed the first generation of the first gods, goddesses, and other mythical creatures who would then bear the succeeding generations.

Among the younger gods that came from Ymir were the brothers Ve, Vili, and Odin. It was in their hands where the great giant fell. These three Norse gods then created the Earth, which they called Midgard. It is the realm that bridges the gap between the land of the gods known as Asgard and the land of the dead, which is Hel.

The Pantheon of Norse Gods

The Norse gods are of three classifications:

- **The Aesir** - These are the gods of the tribes or clans. They represent kingship, craft, and order, among many other things, and Odin and Thor are two of the gods in this classification. These Germanic gods are residents of the realm known as Asgard.

- **The Vanir** - These are the gods of the Earth and the forces of nature who are also the deities of fertility. Among them are Freyr and Freya.

- **The Jotnar** - These are the giants that occupy the realms of Jotunheim and Muspelheim. These beings are in a constant war with the Asgardians, which is why they represent chaos and destruction.

Most people intensely worship four of the deities and mythical creatures populating the nine realms. They are:

- **Odin** - Also known as Woden, Odin is the All-Father, the ruler of all the Aesir and Vanir. He is the most revered but also the most mysterious of all the Norse gods. Most people portray him as a haggard wanderer, relentlessly seeking knowledge despite ruling all Asgard.

Don't be fooled with Odin's always benevolent portrayal in mass media, though, as he is not perfect. He also has a sinister side to him. Odin is depicted as the epitome of battle frenzy. He has provoked countless wars.

- **Thor** - Undoubtedly, Thor is the most well-known of all the Germanic Norse gods, and most of his fame came from modern comics, cartoons, and movies, but modern-day Thor does not resemble his Norse mythology counterpart. Aside from being gruff and wielding the magical hammer Mjolnir, the resemblances stop there.

The actual Thor is a redhead with red eyes, and he rides a chariot pulled by two giant goats. Aside from being the defender of Asgard and the god of the sky and thunder, Thor is also the god of agriculture, fertility, and hallowing.

- **Freyr** - Probably one of the most beloved of all the Norse gods along with his twin sister Freya, Freyr has a unique origin. Unlike most of the other Germanic gods, Freyr came from the Vanir tribe.

Usually portrayed as a large and brawny man with long flowing hair, the Norse hailed him as the topmost god with fertility, and in agriculture, harvests, wealth, peace, and sexual virility. Since the ancient Norse relied heavily on agriculture, many worship Freyr hoping to have a bountiful harvest all the time.

- **Freya/Freyja** - She is the twin sister of Freyr and the Norse goddess of beauty and love. She is also famous for being the goddess of fate and destiny. She and her twin brother Freyr became honorary members of the Aesir after the tribal war between them and the Vanir. According to the Norse religion, Freya could tinker with people's destinies.

Religious Practices

The ancient people who practiced the Germanic pagan religion often held their rituals in or near bodies of water like lakes, bogs, and marshes. They believed that such places are sacred and can let the mortals contact the divine. It is the reason archaeologists find numerous wooden figures depicting people with strongly emphasized sexual features, suggesting that they were offerings to the Norse pagan gods of fertility.

Sacrifices were fundamental elements of Norse/Germanic religion. The ancient people believed that destroying or sending the sacrifice in a place where humans cannot access them is a surefire way for them to reach their intended deities. The ritual burning or throwing of sacrificial objects into lakes became frequent. Festivals also frequently accompanied these rituals - with them all involving copious amounts of eating and drinking.

Often, carved wooden figurines were used for sacrifice, but there were also times when people were offered to the gods by weighing them down using stones and throwing them into boggy marshes. Most of the time, the victims were purported to be witches who brought misfortune to their community. Peat bogs were the preferred sacrificial altar of sorts because the body would not dissolve and get sent to the other world. Instead, it was preserved forever in a state in-between our world and the other world.

At other times, the Norse people would offer their beloved weapons to their gods. Oddly enough, you will not find human remains in the places where weapons are offered up to the gods. Often, the weapons used for sacrifice came from the Norse people's slain enemies, and these were usually sent to Odin.

Modern Germanic/Norse Religion and Practices

If you think that the Norse religion is long gone, then you will be surprised to know that it still exists up to today. You can still find many groups of people around the world but mostly concentrated within Europe and in the Scandinavian isles, who practice a modern form of the pagan religion. They unironically call the practice Heathenry.

Heathens, pertaining to those who practice Heathenry, used to be a derogatory term, and it still is actually. It pertains to the uncivilized societies that have not been converted to Christianity. Heathenry is now a form of a new religious movement that aims to reconstruct the pre-Christian belief systems of the Norse/Germanic tribes and apply them to modern times. Practitioners of Heathenry seek to revive the ancient belief systems using whatever surviving historical source materials they can muster.

Just like the ancient Germanic religion, Heathenry has not unanimously accepted theology. Today's form of Heathenry is polytheistic, just like the ancient pagan religion. It also features a pantheon of gods and goddesses, the same ones that the early Germanic tribes used to worship.

Unlike Christianity, the gods and goddesses of Heathenry are not perfect, omnipotent, and omnipresent. They think of them as having their own strengths and weaknesses. They believe that their gods will one day die like what befell Baldr in Norse mythology.

What is Asatro?

Speaking of the modern Norse religion, it is important to learn about what Asatro is. Asatro refers to the modern term used to define the act of worshipping Norse gods – the ones practiced by the old believers thousands of years ago. This concept does not just focus on the gods. It also aims to worship ancestors and giants. The term is relatively modern and gained recognition only during the 19th century.

The Asatro is divided into kindreds. These refer to local worship groups. Also called stead or garth, kindreds could either be affiliated or not to a national organization. They also consist of hearths, individuals, or families. Kindred members tend to become related through marriage or blood.

Asatro, as the modern version of the Norse religion, also runs based on nine important virtues. Composed of ethical and moral standards derived from various literary and historical sources, Asatro works based on these nine noble virtues that also form a huge part of Norse paganism:

- **Courage** – It encompasses both moral and physical courage. The courage mentioned here is the ability to stand up for your beliefs, especially in terms of what is just and right. This means you have your own persona and are not easily swayed by popular opinion.

- **Truth** – This virtue covers different kinds of truth, including actual and spiritual truth. It is a powerful virtue, which serves as a reminder to everybody of the importance of speaking the truth instead of talking based on what others want to hear.

- **Honor** - It covers your moral compass and reputation. This virtue makes you remember how important it is to be mindful of your words, reputation, and deeds as all those can outlive your human body. This means that people will remember the way you live your life for quite a long time.
- **Fidelity** - This virtue is also another one that people will remember you by. It is all about staying true not only to the Gods you know but also to your kinsmen, community, and spouse. It also revolves around loyalty. This means that letting down a friend, your Gods, or a kindred member also signifies that you turn your back on the whole community and its beliefs and principles.
- **Discipline** - This noble virtue is all about upholding your honor and your other virtues willingly. Note that to be just and ethical, you need to build discipline - strong mental discipline, to be exact. There, your willingness also matters since it is your choice to uphold the virtues you believe in.
- **Hospitality** - The hospitality virtue is not just the simple act of accepting guests with open arms. It is also the way you treat others. You must treat the surrounding people with respect and be willing to be part of your community.
- **Industriousness** - This virtue signifies how important it is to work hard to attain your goals. It requires you to implement hard work in all the things you intend to do, as you owe this not only to yourself but also to the Gods, your family, and your community.
- **Self-Reliance** - This is the eighth noble virtue you must develop to practice Asatro. It is all about your ability to take care of yourself and maintain strong relationships with the deity. Note that while honoring the gods is extremely important, you should also not forget to give both your mind

and body the care they need. In Asatro, you must look for the balance between doing for yourself and doing for others.

- **Perseverance** - last, there is this noble virtue called perseverance. Here, you will need to push onward regardless of all the obstacles that get in your way. If you built this vital virtue, then you would be capable of rising even if you were dealing with defeat. Your perseverance will also let you learn and achieve growth, even if you have committed mistakes and made poor choices along the way.

All these virtues are also among those that most modern Norse believers live by.

Practices of Heathenry

Heathenry celebrates two main rites called blōt and symbel (pronounced as sumble). Practitioners of Heathenry would often hold feasts based around these two main rites, like rites of passage, rites that honor a particular god or gods, and many other forms of celebration.

Originally, a blōt would include the ritual sacrifice of one or more animals to gain the favor of one or more gods or honor their ancestors. After the ritual sacrifice, a feast will be held, allowing the participants of the rite to partake of the meat of the sacrificed animal. Usually, a blōt occurs if the people wish for a particular purpose, like peace, good weather, bountiful crops, or victory.

A modern blōt no longer includes an animal sacrifice, as most people perceive it as too inhumane. It now centers upon offering food, drink, or any other items to the gods, but there will still be a feast after finishing the rite. For outdoor blōts, the items for sacrifice are often thrown into a raging bonfire. But for an indoor blōt, the participants reserve a place setting for the god or ancestor they wish to honor.

A symbol is a rite where there is a drinking horn or two filled with mead or any appropriate alcoholic beverage. After having the drinks blessed and sanctified according to Heathenistic practices, the practitioners will pass the horns around, and each will take a drink. The first round of toasts is usually offered to the gods, the second round for the ancestors, and the third is for whatever the assembled Heathens agree upon.

Besides giving offerings to the gods, most Heathens leave small gifts for the domestic "hidden folk," like the wights who live in their yards. Many Heathens have a special bowl where they place their offerings. Some even have a small altar in their garden. Often, Heathens will make a small offering for their house wight whenever they are baking bread or brewing their own mead. They do this for good luck, and to shoo away the negative energy that can spoil their produce.

You also need to be respectful towards your house wight. You have to respect their space, which you can do simply by keeping your home clean. Always do your best to be in the good graces of your hidden folk.

Morality and Ethics

Although the name Heathen has always been associated with being uncivilized and without morals, that is the opposite of what real practitioners of the religion stand for. Heathens base their ethical and moral views on the actions by the characters in old Norse sagas. Their ethics focus mainly on the ideals of honor, hospitality, the virtue of hard work, courage, and integrity. They also strongly focus on family bonds.

The Heathen community expects members to keep their word all the time, most especially if they made a sworn oath. The main reason can be pointed to a strong individualist ethos that focuses mainly on personal responsibility. "We are our deeds" is a common motto used within the community. Most Heathenry practitioners reject the concept of sin. They believe that being guilted for your past actions is more destructive than it is useful.

Magic and Seership

It is common for members of the ancient Norse religion to partake in the practice of magic and divination. Every community has at least one person who practices the mystic arts. In modern Heathenry, many still believe and practice magic and divination. They are even actively reviving many practices used by the ancient Germanic cultures.

Practices that modern Heathens are actively reviving include the creation of runic talismans and the chanting of charms (galdor). Many are also rediscovering the Northern European divination practice called "seidh." "Oracular seidh" is an ancient ritual where a seer will answer questions or give advice to the participants.

Many modern Heathens also use runes to foretell the future. Foretelling might not be the right word here. One can use runes as oracles for advice. They give hints on how to find the answers to your questions, but it is you who will ultimately need to figure out the details. However, it is important for rune casters to have excellent intuition.

Runic divination is not fortunetelling per se. The runes will only give you a means of analyzing your path and determining the possible outcomes if you stay on the same course. Practitioners of rune divination do not particularly believe in predestination. According to them, your future is not set in stone. You can change your outcome by changing the present.

Chapter 2: The Divine Gift of Futhark

Now that you have had a quick introduction to Heathenry or, in other words, the modern Norse religion, it is time for you to learn more about the practice of divination and reading runes. Before you can learn rune divination, you need to understand how to read runes. The talismans you will be using later are all inscribed using a runic alphabet known as the Futhark, and this chapter will teach you all about this ancient writing system.

The Elder Futhark

In modern pop culture, the Norse/Germanic runes always seem to have mystical and mysterious properties. With that in mind, you can see their symbolism often being used in fantasy video games and tabletop games. Wiccan practitioners also use runes for their ceremonies and rituals, pretty much like modern Heathens use them.

The Germanic tribes of the Scandinavian isles had always used runes (well before Christianity came onto their shores). After most of the population were forced to convert to Christianity, runes and other old Heathen practices became known as pagan. It directly opposes

Christianity. Hence, it was outlawed and almost wiped out of existence. The Christian colonizers could not eradicate the Germanic religion completely, and it only added intrigue and mystique to the runes.

The Runic alphabet, also known as the Futhark, is the system of writing used by the ancient Germanic tribes. The name came from the first six letters of the runes, namely F, U, TH, A, R, and K. It is pretty much the same way as when the alphabet came from alpha and beta, the first two letters of the Greek alphabet.

There are no clear explanations as to why the Futhark runes are arranged in such a peculiar way. Although no one knows the real answer, many experts believe that it is a form of the mnemonic function to make it easier to memorize the letters.

Mythical Origin of the Runes

Odin, the All-Father, has always been on a never-ending quest for more knowledge and wisdom. He is so relentless that he will sacrifice anything to get more knowledge, as evidenced by his one eye. He sacrificed his other eye in exchange for more wisdom, but that is another story.

Odin's discovery of the Germanic runes had him do many inconceivable things on himself. It is all thanks to his seemingly unquenchable thirst for understanding the myriad of mysteries in the cosmos. Also, it is a testament to his unshakeable will.

After Odin and his brothers defeated the giant Ymir, he created the realm of man, which he called Midgard. After finishing the creation of the Nine Realms, he hoped and wished to acquire more than enough wisdom so he could use it to watch over them.

It prompted him to send out Thought and Memory, two of his ravens, into various worlds throughout the day. The roles of his ravens include communicating with all creatures, whether or not they were dead or alive. They would come back at night to tell Odin about all the information they gathered during their exploration.

Odin continued with that setup until eventually, he tired of it. He felt unsatisfied with the specific manner through which he acquired wisdom and knowledge. This motivated him to look for and collect all his desired information by himself. This decision led to his seemingly endless pursuit of wisdom and knowledge.

Odin had a strong urge and desire to acquire knowledge, so he visited Mimir. He was the wisest man of the entire Aesir. Odin's wish was to acquire knowledge by drinking from Mimir's well. The reason was this powerful well held one root of Yggdrasil containing all information about the Nine Realms.

Odin relayed this intention to Mimir, but the latter informed him that to fulfill his intention, he had to sacrifice something. His sacrifice should be substantial and fitting for a god-like him. Odin was then asked to sacrifice one eye, and he never even once hesitated to do so. His hunger for knowledge made him agree to dig his left eye out and then give it to Mimir, but even after that incident, Odin still seemed insatiable with all his acquired knowledge.

He continued his exploration and quest until he learned about the magical runes and their secrets. He got intensely interested in them upon learning these mysterious symbols can give users complete control over the forces of nature, but he also knew the need to make a huge sacrifice to master the runes and understand them deeply. He knew that he might have to endure extreme suffering to where he would be on the brink of death.

He was prepared to do all that just to satisfy his need for knowledge. It was at this moment when he stabbed his side with a sword, then hung himself on the Yggdrasil's branches. He stayed that way for nine days without eating, drinking, or sleeping. He discovered the runes and their individual powers and mysteries successfully after getting close to death.

Odin also realized how useful the runes were when it came to doing even those seemingly impossible acts, like talking to the dead, healing those who are sick, predicting what will happen, and calling upon and calming storms. With this newly acquired knowledge, he had a strong desire to share it with the world. This promoted him to carve the first 18 runes in stone, wood, and bone. He even did the carving in the claws of a wolf and the beak of an eagle, too. After carving, he relayed all these items to everyone who lived in Midgard.

The Connection Between Wood and the Runes

The Futhark originated from the runes passed down by Odin, but the runes themselves retained their original powers. The ancient Norse Vikings and other Germanic tribes used runes whenever they wanted to talk to their fallen relatives or acquaintances. They also used them for protection and peace.

Aside from that, most also discovered that the runes were useful for divination and contacting beings who existed on the other planes of existence. They used different materials to draw the different runes on, including wood (most especially oak, beech, and pine), bones, shells, paper, or stone. Most believe that runes are more powerful if you create them yourself, instead of using the ones that other people made.

The most common material used for rune making is wood. It is mainly due to the wooden element's importance in Norse mythology. For instance, the Tree of Life, Yggdrasil, sustains the Nine Worlds from its branches. Most of the Norse artifacts with runes inscribed on them are made of wood.

Futhark in Britain

At around 400 to 500 AD, three Germanic tribes from Scandinavia, the Angles, Saxons, and the Jutes, invaded Britain. Along with their culture, they brought along the Futhark. As time went on, they modified the Futhark into the 33-letter "Futhorc" so it could accommodate the unique sounds that came with the Old English language, the language spoken by the Anglo-Saxons.

According to linguists, the "Futhorc" is evidence of the phonological change where the Old English long /a/ vowel evolved into the /o/ vowel sound. Initially, the Futhark/Futhorc writing system seemed to thrive in Britain. But it declined, and eventually, it almost disappeared with the spread of the Latin alphabet.

Futhorc went on the decline during the 9th century AD, and by the 10th century, missionaries converted all the Germanic tribes to Christianity. With the dissolution of their old way of life, their culture and the Futhark alphabet also slowly diminished.

Modern Believers

Even after a thousand years of finishing the Viking age, Thor and Odin, and the other gods and goddesses in the Norse religion, were still strong, with many people still believing in them. When Christianity was introduced, the old Nordic religion somehow declined or disappeared, but there is still a significant number of people who practice it. After Christianity was introduced, the Norse religion was practiced secretly. Some even practiced it while hiding under the cloak of Christianity.

Presently, you can still find many people from various parts of the world who believe in the Norse religion and magic. Around 500 to 1,000 people in Denmark still have a strong faith in this religion up to the present day. These people still worship the ancient gods.

Like what the Vikings did, most modern believers meet up openly. It is when they worship and praise the Gods they believe in and give offerings; among the rituals they do to honor their Gods are drinking a toast and eating a feast. For instance, some offer a toast to the Gods of fertility if their intentions include prosperity and an abundant harvest.

The toast could also be personal, such as when a woman wants to get pregnant or search for eternal love. For those struggling, they can praise Thor so they will become stronger. They can also invoke Odin to gain wisdom.

One thing to note about the modern belief and faith in the Norse Gods is that it does not serve as a direct succession of what the Vikings believed in. Generally, it focuses more on reinterpreting and reviving the old religion. The reason could be the limited written sources regarding this subject.

What Can Runes Be Used For?

Are you curious about the things that runes can help you with? As suggested by their historical origins, you can use them for many things, but unless you are a Norse god, you may not be able to use them to control the weather or talk to the dead just yet. However, you will still find them useful for several reasons and situations.

One specific situation where you can use runes is when you need guidance. - maybe a time when you find yourself in a rough patch in your life. This is called divination, which differs from fortune-telling, as it will not tell you a straight answer on how events will unfold. The runes will let you know about the different variables that may happen and what possible outcomes your actions can bring.

Runes will hint toward answers, but they will still let you work toward finding the details. With that in mind, have a keen intuition when using runes. Rune readers acknowledge that the future is not set in stone. This means you still have the power to make your own decisions that can change the outcomes.

If you do not like what the runes are saying about your future, you are free not to accept it and do the appropriate actions to prevent the divination from happening. You still have the chance to change your direction or go on a different path.

You can also use runes when you find yourself where you have limited information only before making a practical decision. It is always necessary to use your intuition to make sense of what they are telling you.

Again, casting runes differs from actual fortune-telling. The idea behind the way you use runes is that your conscious and subconscious minds focus on them whenever you ask them questions. When you cast them, your sub-conscious may have decided for you. The runes are just around to help make it clearer.

Some people believe that you can ask runes only about the issues that bother you specifically. Others believe that it is fine to ask specific questions. Regardless of what you ask, it is best to think of your query clearly. Remember that as you are casting your runes.

Also, remember that reading runes is not an exact science. You will not see a clear future outcome, nor will you get a clear answer to your question. Rune reading is more about using your intuition to look for possible outcomes.

Other Uses for Runes

Runes are not just tools used for divination but also powerful relics you can use for other purposes. Here are a couple of their other famous uses:

Jewelry

You can carve the rune symbols onto your jewelry. Here, you can use any precious metals you like. It is even possible for you to carve the runes onto gemstones if you want to. You may use your imagination as to what you inscribe runes onto. There is no wrong way of doing it if your intentions are in the right place. Don't worry about them backfiring. You can rest assured knowing that even if you use the runes improperly, they will only be ineffective instead of being dangerous.

Talismans

While inscribing runes onto jewelry is a passive method of using them (other people may view them as decorative designs), talismans are more obvious in their usage. These are large medallions with runic inscriptions. They also often have a large stone in the middle.

Heathen practitioners consider rune talismans as conscious and alive, which is why you can keep them permanently or make them in such a way you can release them once their intended purpose manifests. You can make that possible by burying the runes in the Earth, so they can return to nature.

Making the Best Runes

Historically, rune makers will use their blood or that of a sacrificial animal to pigment their runes, allegedly empowering them even more, but it is not really a requirement. As a matter of fact, you can use any kind of paint or ink you like, especially if you are the squeamish type who can't stand the sight of blood.

Consider timing when creating a rune. There, consider the phase of the moon at that moment. For instance, to create runes that represent the growth and accomplishment of goals, make them during a waxing moon. But the best time to create runes designed to eliminate or dispel is when there is a waning moon.

The most basic and easiest way to pick rune inscriptions is to write them horizontally. In the old days, rune inscriptions were done in odd numbers, but if you are not a fan of the traditional method, you can just choose any number you feel like using, but remember that sometimes, the "less is more" concept is more applicable. Rune inscriptions are among those times. Think of rune inscription as telling a story, so you are describing the outcome you want.

Some rune makers also enjoy chanting or singing the name of each rune every time they are creating them. You can also do that. The important thing is that you focus on charging the runes with your personal intentions while you are creating them.

How Does Rune Casting Work?

Again, casting runes differs from actual fortune-telling. The idea behind the way you use runes is that your conscious and subconscious minds focus on them whenever you ask the runes questions. When you cast them, your subconscious has decided for you. The runes just help to make it clearer.

What Sort of Runes Do You Need?

You can use different materials for runes. Among the most popular ones are stone, crystals, bones, metal, and wood. If you are just a beginner at reading runes and are still getting a feel for it, then using a basic/simple rune set will do. If you have been rune casting for years, you can get a special set for yourself.

If you feel like there is a certain attraction between you and a certain rune, like it is speaking out to you, then you should get it. When you purchase a set of runes, they usually come with a pamphlet explaining what each rune represents and the different options you can interpret them. It would be even better if you carved out your own set of runes. You can use crystals, animal bones, wood, or even metal for that purpose if you so wish.

Runes you make yourself have more power inside of them than pre-made ones. Regardless of the material or who made them, the thing that matters the most is what you do with them.

Chapter 3: The Fundamentals of Divination

Now that you have a bit of understanding about runes and their mystical and historical origins, you can learn how you can use them. Since using the mystical properties of runes, like weather control and talking to the dead, among many others, is still out of the hands of mere mortals, you can learn how to use them for divination. This process is also called rune casting.

What is Rune Casting?

Rune casting is a method of oracular divination, where the user lays out or casts the runes. It can either be in a specific pattern, or you can throw them randomly. It is a way for people to gain guidance on how to deal with their problems or face their situations. Basically, it gives a way for people to make sensible decisions.

Runes will not give you an exact answer to your inquiries. They cannot tell you when or how you will die, nor will it let you know who you will marry and when. You will not also receive any advice from runes. You can't expect them to tell you you should quit your job and become a professional gamer. They will not advise you to dump your cheating spouse and take the kids with you.

Runes will suggest the possible outcomes of your decision. Put simply, they will only give you hints. You will need to use your critical thinking skills and your intuition to figure out the best course of action for your situation.

Like with other kinds of divination methods, the answers from runic divination are not final. If you do not like what the runes are telling you, just change what you are doing and choose another path. You are still the master of your own destiny. The runes are just there as your guide.

How Easy is it to Interpret Runes?

Only a few people can pick up the art of rune divination on the first try. It will take time before you can call yourself a master of the art. Usually, when you buy a set of runes, it comes with an instructional pamphlet that shows how you can interpret them. You can consult many books and videos to learn as much as you can about runes, but they will most likely not be enough.

For many, learning how to interpret runes accurately will be a lifelong affair. Still, it can be an uplifting experience. You will also be delighted to know that eventually, reading them will get easier, especially if you practice.

If you have good intuition, it is much easier to figure out what the runes are potentially telling you. If you are unsure about the rune's message, don't worry, as it might not just relate to your current situation. Try to preserve as much of the information the runes are telling you. Write down the details of your divination, especially the ones whose details you are unsure of, and then find out if the details become more relevant later.

Even rune casters with many years of experience under their belt still admit that they do not understand the meanings of the runes they cast sometimes. Some even have to wait for weeks or months after the casting for answers to come to them.

The Importance of Meditating Before Rune Casting

Whether or not you are a beginner at rune casting or have been doing it for years, you have most likely tried different techniques to improve your rune reading accuracy. A few techniques you tried may have worked, while others did nothing. While you have learned quite a lot of new things, your rune reading prowess seems unchanged.

One method that seems to work for many rune casters – and most likely for you – is meditation. Why does meditation seem to work so well? The following reasons might explain it.

It Calms Your Mind, Letting You Think Clearly

Having a calm and relaxed mind will allow you to clear your thoughts and minimize any stress you are experiencing somehow. You need a clear mind because you will be trying to read the runes in a focused and deliberate manner. It is important to look at the runes you cast and try to make sense of them as best as you can. Note you are trying to figure out what is coming. Just doing these things is already difficult, and it gets even harder when you have a stressed-out mind.

For instance, after a stressful day at work or school, you come home, and a million thoughts are racing through your mind. You sit down and try to cast your runes, but the only thing going through your mind is the pile of paperwork you need to sift through at work or the looming test on Monday. Your mind is obviously not focused on the runes, which can lead to messing up your readings if there is anything there.

It Allows You to Access a Higher Level of Thought

What is a higher level of thought? It means you have complete focus on whatever task you have at hand. It is like you have tuned out the rest of the world and can only see and hear the task in front of you.

There are different levels of consciousness that the human mind can reach. The higher the level, the more awareness your mind has. You become more sensitive to the things that are happening around you and in your lower levels of consciousness. It is a great help for rune casters because a focused mind allows them to visualize things they could not visualize before.

It Gives You More Control Over Your Body and Mind

If you are like most rune casters, then you have most likely tried to find the best place in your home to do your readings, but you can't seem to find a setting completely quiet and free of distractions. You cannot completely escape distractions; the only thing you can do realistically is to train your mind so they will have no negative effects.

Meditation will help you train your mind so it can acclimatize itself to any situation that may happen. It will not make your mind completely blank nor numb to outside stimuli, but it will make you more mindful. Mindfulness means that your mind recognizes that there will be distractions wherever you go, but instead of letting these thoughts create a state of stress, you can acknowledge them and accept that they are there.

It promotes ease in willing your way through the distractions and focusing on your task, which, in this case, is rune casting. With mindfulness meditation, you can cast your runes even in the pouring rain. Any form of distraction will not bother you in the slightest.

How Meditation Can Help with Readings

Suppose you can place yourself into a higher level of thought due to meditation. There, you will immediately discover that, even if you are not actively meditating, your senses are still more aware than ever. Every time you open your senses to the everyday world, you exercise and continuously train your mind to see things differently. You will have other perspectives where you can base your decisions.

Because you are more in tune with your surroundings, you can easily pick up the smaller details you may have otherwise missed, helping you make sense of the runes better. For instance, when you sit down with a person for a rune reading, you can get a grasp of his or her personality. You can read other people better so you can give them a more accurate interpretation of the runes.

Here is a sample scenario. You have a friend who is going for a job interview next week, and he wants to know if he will get the job. Being his friend, you already know that he is the kind of person who will tense up during an interview but is also very qualified.

You also know the job your friend is interviewing for involves dealing with other people, so it is important for him to work on his people skills. In that case, you may cast your runes. Perhaps Uruz is the most important. Uruz is a rune for power –but it is one out of people's control. It can also mean that success is nearby.

Typically, you can tell your friend that success is near, but it comes with a power he has no control over. Also, you are not sure when this power will come. If you meditate before the reading and are in a more mindful state, you can sense your friend's attitude about the job. If you feel that your friend is in control, it is highly likely that the power without control comes with the job.

Preparing for Rune Casting

Do you think that you are already ready to cast runes? If you are, then know there are still a couple more things you need to do to bring yourself to the right headspace. Rune castings and readings require you to be comfortable and prepared before you start.

As a disclaimer, these tips are not requirements for a rune reading. The only thing you need will be a set of runes. You know yourself better than anyone else, so you are the only one who can say what makes you comfortable before doing a reading.

However, here are a few suggestions depending on certain key factors:

Time of Day

Some rune casters believe that castings should be done only during the day. It should always be outside with the sun shining brightly. But some say that the best time is just before midnight. It is the time when the veil separating this world and the other world is at its thinnest. It means it is easier to communicate with the spirits.

Some also say there is a way to calculate which time is best to do a reading, depending on the questions you will be asking. The time you do the reading will depend on your preferences. There is no evidence that proves one way is better than the others. The better thing to do is to do your castings during different times of the day and see which times suit you best.

Weather

The weather plays a huge role when rune casting and reading. It was mentioned earlier that some casters prefer sunny days rather than overcast or rainy days. The main reason is that the weather can influence a person's mood. For instance, most people feel inexplicably sad when the sky is grey or when it is raining, and they feel more positive when the sun is shining. Some people also feel more comfortable when it is overcast outside or raining. The most important thing here is to schedule your casting during a time when the weather and your mood are at their best.

Surroundings

Your surroundings also play a huge part when you are rune casting. The reason could be each location has its own unique energy field. For instance, you may not want to cast somewhere with plenty of power lines or cellular towers as the energy they give off may interfere with your own.

Also, consider the kind of people who are around you. It is best to avoid those who are skeptical or do not believe in the power of the runes outright. If you surround yourself with highly skeptical people, they will influence your own feelings about the runes. You may even doubt yourself, thus resulting in a poor and inaccurate reading.

Casting Set-Up

If you are rune casting outdoors, then the setup you have to go for should be simple and basic. You just need to face the sun, lay out your casting cloth (if you will be using one), place your pillow, and then sit on it. Across from you, place your mearmots and a piece of paper that contains the question you wish to ask the runes (optional).

Put your hand inside the rune pouch and mix up the runes. Gather the number of runes you need depending on the casting type, then toss them onto the casting cloth or right in front of you.

If you fancy casting indoors, then you can use a couple of setups. First, find a space that is big enough so you can lay out your casting cloth with nothing in its way. The cloth should also be flat and not bunched up.

If possible, sit facing east or wherever the sun's position is at the time. If you are casting at night, set your layout so you face the moon. If these setups are impossible in your home, just lay the cloth so nothing obstructs it – that will be fine.

A Quick Overview of the Casting Procedure

Now, onto casting the runes. Some magical traditions do the process by casting or tossing the runes onto a white cloth. The cloth provides a clear background for reading the runes and a magical boundary extremely useful during the casting process.

Some casters do it directly on the ground. As the one who will be doing the casting, you have the freedom to pick the method you want. Once the casting session ends, get a small box or pouch where you can store them.

You can cast runes using any of the many methods available. Each one of them is as valid as the next. There are a couple of layouts that are currently popular with modern rune casters.

Like other divination methods, rune casting basically addresses one particular issue and lets you look for the things that could influence it from your past and present. For instance, you may want to do a 3-rune cast by pulling three one at a time from the pouch. You can then place them side-by-side on a white cloth.

The first rune you pulled out represents the general overview of your situation. The second one is for the challenges and obstacles in your way, while the last one gives you the potential paths you can take in response.

Here is how a basic rune casting session would usually start:

- Lay out your runes on the cloth, all facing up to make sure that the set is complete. After that, you can put them back inside the pouch.

- Place your hand inside the pouch and mix them up as best as you can. While doing so, concentrate on your question.

- Pick up a couple of runes that will depend on the casting method you chose and toss them onto the cloth.

- Use the runes that landed face up to do your reading. If you do not have enough runes facing upward to do your reading, you can choose to re-cast and start over again, re-cast the runes that landed face-down or leave the spaces in the spread blank.

How to Pick the Runes from the Casting Cloth

Once the runes are on the casting cloth, the next thing that may cross your mind is how to figure out which ones to pick up. Fortunately, there are a couple of ways to do so. The first involves picking a spot on the cloth before you cast them. Then pick up the rune closest to it for the first spot on the spread. After that, pick the one closest next. Continue doing so until all the spaces in your spread are full.

Another way is to imagine a line running down the center of the casting cloth and then pick up the face-up rune that lands closest to it first. If two runes are somewhat the same distance from the line, pick the one closest to you first. The spots in your spread are full; the next step is to read them and figure out their meanings.

Chapter 4: The Runemaster's Tools

Now that you have the basic gist of rune casting and reading, it is time for you to prepare your own tools for divination. The primary tools that all rune casters need to have are the runes themselves. There, you can choose to either make the runes on your own or buy them.

Making Your Own Runes

If you are just learning about runes, making your own set is a good way for you to memorize each runic symbol. Painting or carving the symbols onto your desired media can serve as a sort of meditation, which is also helpful in infusing more of your energy into your runes.

Depending on how skilled you are with your hands and your level of adeptness at crafts, and the materials you have to work with, making your own rune sets can be a good outlet for your creativity. If you create your own Elder Futhark runes, then you will need 24 similar-sized objects for your rune tiles (25 if you will be including a wyrd rune).

You can usually find the perfect materials in your local craft store. To go through it in the same way as the ancient Nords did, you can find the materials you will need right in your backyard.

The great thing about buying from the craft store is that you can easily get uniformly shaped tiles, as opposed to going to your local stream and spending hours searching for pebbles roughly the same size and shape.

Searching through nature for the materials for your runes makes the process more spiritual. The runes you make will also be highly personal and unique. Making your own runes has these pros and cons:

Pros

- It allows you to build a more personal connection with your runes.
- It gives you the chance to exercise your creativity since you will be the one to create a unique set of runes.
- More budget-friendly compared to buying them

Cons

- Unless you are skilled and have the right materials and equipment, you might not get runes that are as beautiful as the commercially available ones.

Buying Commercially Available Runes

Meanwhile, a lot of specialty shops and websites nowadays offer pre-made rune sets. You can just purchase them if you do not want to deal with the hassle of making one on your own. Pre-made ones are often constructed helped by techniques and materials hard to replicate by anyone. It may even be more challenging to replicate them if you are not the crafty type.

You can get runes that are laser-engraved, especially if you want the inscriptions to be permanent. You can also find those with beautiful inlays. If you do not have the necessary tools, equipment, and skills to do such meticulously crafted items, it is better to invest your money in pre-made ones. It is especially true if you feel that a certain rune set is calling out to you.

Usually, commercially available sets contain the twenty-four runes popularized by the Futhark. Most of these runes also feature a wyrd or blank rune, which serves as a wild card. As it is pre-made, you can expect each one also to have its own decorative box or drawstring pouch. Most also contain instructions so users will not have a hard time familiarizing themselves with the runes and the basics of using them.

Note, though, that just because these extra items come with the runes, you are under no obligation to use them and the specific instructions about their usage. Rune reading techniques vary, and no two casters use the same exact method of going about it.

Pros

- Offers several options
- Several unique and beautifully made runes are available for sale – Some are so unique that you simply cannot replicate them.
- Always uniform in size and design

Cons

- It will be challenging to build a strong spiritual bond with your runes since you just bought them.

Materials

Some materials that make great runes include wood nickels, sawn-off slices from a tree branch, kiln-fired clay tiles, or glass aquarium rocks. Basically, anything that is small and uniform in size will work well.

Now, also consider the durability of the material. Some people used flat rocks they got from riverbeds only to discover later that they were fragile sedimentary rocks that tend to chip and disintegrate easily. Uncured wood will crack and split along the grain.

Painted symbols on a smooth surface would usually chip off when the runes scrape against each other in the pouch. It will take trial-and-error before you can find a material that will be durable enough to last at least a year or two of constant rune readings.

The following are suggestions on the kind of material that you can use to make your rune set.

Bone - You can make runes out of animal bones cleaned and left out in the sun to bleach and dry. You can also use these bones if you are a collector of these materials. With that, you will have ready materials for making the runes, specifically the skeletal remains of animals.

When planning to use animal bones, a wise tip is to look for the thickest and densest ones. The reason is that thick and dense bones are highly recommended for rune-making. Upon research, you may also realize how easy it will be to work on a rune if you use femurs.

If you are not a collector and you are just planning to purchase the bones for the runes, then be prepared to look for the ones from water buffaloes, as these are ideal. The reason is that the commercially available ones are made from such animals. These bones are also known for being by-products of dairy and meat farming in Asia.

Antlers – The deer antlers' cross-sections are also great materials for rune-making. The neat thing is that you need not hunt deer just to get their antlers. Early winter is when the rutting season ends, and male deer will shed their antlers. You will usually find the discarded antlers near the base of the trees in the woods inhabited by the deer.

To connect with the Stag energy, then deer antlers are the best choice for making your runes. Keep them away from your dog, as deer antler runes look a lot like dog kibble!

Wood - You can use any kind of wood you want for making your rune set. You can stick to the types that, according to folklore, have magical properties, like Ash, Elder, and Oak. You are still free to pick any wood with a personal significance, like the branches of the tree in your backyard you planted when you were young.

If you are using fresh woods from trees, then make sure to dry them thoroughly first to prevent them from splitting. You need not go through this step if you will be buying your wood commercially since those have been kiln-dried already.

Stone - Heathenry practitioners say that any rune made of stone is already a modern invention. Some even believe that the only materials designed for rune-making are bones and wood. It is just a misconception as you can work on any material you can think of. If you can inscribe your runes, then it is all good, so the stone is also a great idea.

One probable reason wood and bone were used back in the day is that they were readily available and relatively easy to carve compared to stones. You can use precious or semi-precious gems or just ordinary pebbles to make your runes. It does not necessarily need to be expensive. Gemstone runes are undoubtedly beautiful, and they have a nice heft to them, making them nice to cast.

You can also choose gemstones known for having magical properties to bolster the powers of the runes even further. For instance, you can make them out of jasper for courage and hematite for protection.

Ceramic - You can also find runes made from clay, either air-dried, oven-baked, or fired in a kiln. Of the three, the kiln-fired tiles are the most durable. Ceramic tiles are the most popular with DIY casters because they are the easiest to paint or carve.

Aside from that, this material seems to connect well with the Earth element. You can buy pre-made ceramic tiles you can paint or engrave. You can use broken floor tiles or pots. Just re-shape them to your preference.

Glass and Pewter - Glass and pewter runes are somewhat specialty items, making them hard to come by. The trouble with using glass beads and pewter beads is that they can be hard to paint, as their surfaces are too smooth for the paint to stay onto them properly.

The only way to inscribe runes on them is by etching (sandblasting or acid etching) or by carving. Both methods require special equipment, skill, and steady hands. Even though these materials are difficult to work with, the results will be more than worth the extra effort.

Are there certain materials you should not make into runes? The answer is there is no limit as to what you can use. The important thing about making runes you have to know is that you have to do it with the utmost respect. Odin hung half-dead on Yggdrasil for nine days and nights just to gain the knowledge of the runes.

With that in mind, it would seem disrespectful just to carve the symbol onto cheap Styrofoam and call it a rune. The least you can do is put effort into making your runes presentable and choosing the best materials for your intended purpose.

Size and Shape

Now that you have a handle on the specific materials you can use, it is time to think about the size and shape of the runes you will be making. Most runes, especially the ones in the form of gemstones, are usually around half an inch in diameter, which is too small for practical rune readers.

If you want your runes to be easy to read and feel comfortable in your hands, then you should get bigger ones or make them a bit bigger, like ¾-inch to 1-inch in diameter. This size is also beneficial if you will mostly do readings for others.

Runes come in different sizes and shapes, even when they are in the same set. If you plan to use the blind draw method of rune casting often, then it is important for your runes to have roughly the same size and shapes. This can help prevent making biased draws.

Should your runes be flat, round, symmetrical, or asymmetrical? Rounded runes feel good in the hands when drawing from a pouch, but they have the tendency to roll around too much when you cast them onto the casting cloth. If you are thinking of setting lines or grids with your runes, go with tiles or at least flat circular stones.

Another thing you must consider is whether you intend to read reversed runes. Reversals give different meanings to runes that landed face-down or upside-down. It's hard to tell if a rounded rune is lying face down or on its side. Certain runes also look the same upside-down and right-side-up. If you are dealing with such issues, it would be best for you to use asymmetrical runes and memorize the right orientation of each.

Inscribing the Runes

You can inscribe the Futhark letters onto your medium of choice. Take note, though, that some are more difficult than the rest. Nevertheless, they will still produce beautiful and lasting designs.

Here are just a few of the different ways to inscribe the runes:

Paints/Ink

Most DIY rune casters like to use paints or ink to mark their runes. It is essential to choose the right pigment based on the material you will be using. For instance, if you will be using stones, use acrylic paint as it is the only type that can adhere to stone surfaces.

You can also use different ink markers to write the runes onto the stones. It is the easiest and quickest method for making runes, but it also seems to have the lowest rank as to their durability. Speaking of durability, you will need to put a layer or two of clear varnish to protect the writing and make them last.

Carving

If you want something permanent, rather than simply painting or writing the runes on the surface, then be prepared to carve or engrave the Futhark letters into the tiles. Granted, these methods will need more skill, and if you are inexperienced, you may even cut your hands if you are not careful. Even if they don't come out perfectly, they will still look much better compared to painted runes. Aside from that, you can be assured that it will last a lot longer.

Wood-Burning

This method involves a soldering iron or a true wood-burning wand. It requires the use of a small electronic heating element over the surface of the wood, leaving a burnt, charred line on the surface. The charred line will not be easy to erase unless you sand off a lot of material from the surface of the wood.

You can also use this technique on bone tiles, but you must do it in a well-ventilated area because it may create noxious fumes.

Chapter 5: Rune Preparation: From Cleansing to Empowering

Do you want your runes to work as efficiently as they did when you first made and used them? Then you need to take good care of them, but unlike taking care of other kinds of accessories, maintaining runes does not just entail cleaning them the orthodox way. It entails cleansing and charging them, and you will be learning more about these tasks in this chapter.

Note that runes can be powerful tools, especially when you treat them with care and respect. You will need to cleanse and empower them, especially if they are still new or many people have already touched them.

One thing to remember is that runes are private and personal items, and their owners should be the only ones who keep and see them. You can place them on your desk or in your workspace. It could also be somewhere near your bed.

By keeping them close, you are letting them tune into your personal energy, leading to clearer and more concise rune readings. If you are using them often for reading other people, you will need to cleanse them more often.

Cleansing

There are many ways for you to cleanse your runes. You can choose whatever takes your fancy, but the most important thing is you do it often and regularly. Cleansing is even more important between uses or when you accidentally surround them with another person's energy for too long.

Here are ways to cleanse your runes so they can work properly once again:

- Laying them out at night, or early in the morning, and leaving them out for at least 24 hours.

- Smudging - This method involves passing them through the smoke of smoldering herbs that contain purifying properties primarily designed to cleanse them. If you live somewhere where even a small fire can make your neighbors panic, you can substitute the herbs for a white candle.

- Using natural flowing water, you can also cleanse them using natural flowing water, like a creek or a nearby stream. Never use tap water for cleansing as it has gone through numerous treatment processes, but if you have a bit of rainwater saved in a container in your home, you can use that instead.

Empowering

You can empower your runes simply by keeping them close. You can do so by always carrying them in your pocket or bag. Another way to do it is to keep them within your personal space. That way, they can tune themselves to your personal energy.

Here are other tips you can use:

- Place them outside so the sun can bless them - Just leave the runes outside at the crack of dawn, then bring them back into your home just before dusk.

- Bury your rune set into the soil - You can either bury them in one single pile or put them in a pouch and then bury them. You can dig them up after at least a week has passed.

On the other hand, you can also perform a small but intricate cleansing ceremony. First, cast a circle to chase away any negative energy, then cleanse the space and yourself using the smoke from a smoldering pile of sage. Lay down your casting cloth in the middle of the circle and your runes for cleansing.

Bless the runes with the elements. In this part, you can choose whatever has meaning for you. For instance, for the earth element, sprinkle rock salt. Pass them through the smoke of the sage for the air element. Sprinkle rainwater over them for the water element.

Finally, pass them through the flame of a lit red candle for the fire element. After you finish with the elements, hold each rune tightly in your right hand to imbue each with your spirit.

If you usually use the runes to guide others, it is best to cleanse them before and after every use. Also, it is advisable to re-empower your runes every full moon.

The Proper Way to Store Your Runes

You can store your rune set in a bag, preferably made of a natural material. You also may use any pouch you fancy. You can place them in a wooden box.

Most rune casters use casting cloths, and it is common to find them paired with a particular rune set. If you will be using a casting cloth, it is best to stay consistent with its color and/or material when switching cloths. Doing so will let the runes get in tune with the casting cloth and vice versa.

Like the runes themselves, you should also regularly cleanse the item where you store them because it is essentially their home.

Empowering Yourself

When you continually work with your runes, you will gradually learn more about nature's power. You will understand your place in the universe, allowing you to experience growth in all aspects.

Nature teaches you about maintaining balance and being in harmony. By regularly communing with nature and the elements within, you cannot help but feel enlightened. You feel empowered, as well. Do it regularly, and you will find a true connection with the Universe.

Aside from communing with nature, you can also wear runic symbols on your person to empower yourself. Runes give out powerful vibrations that can serve as protection against harm. They will attract their specific qualities toward your life. Wearing a rune around your neck, like a talisman, will subject your entire being to it and all its related influences.

How to Consecrate Runes

If you just bought or made a new set of runes, or have been using it for a while already, then you should consecrate it first before using it again. Aside from re-energizing your rune set, it will also make your readings more uniform and accurate.

Consecration means to make something holy. When you consecrate your runes, you are turning them from regular stones or tiles into sacred tools for divination.

The great thing about runes is that you can re-consecrate them infinitely. If you realize that your readings have become less clear or accurate as of late, then you will need to consecrate them as soon as you can. You also have to do the consecration if you have not used your runes for a long time and they do not work like they used to anymore.

One thing to remember about consecrating runes is that you are not just purifying and preparing them for use but also creating a spiritual link between them and you. It is the reason you need not be a psychic to use runes. The runes themselves will serve as the bridge between you and the divine.

If you know how to read the runic symbols, you become a sort of interpreter to the divine. You can use them to gain guidance from the other realms in the universe. When you cast and read them, you will discover that they tell a sort of story. You will discover patterns and trends you can use to figure out your next best course of action.

By consecrating your rune set and yourself in the process, you are helping yourself to open up to the messages/story hidden in the runes. It is true whether or not you use them for yourself or if you like to give readings to other people.

Even though you do not have to be a psychic to read runes, your perception will increase. It will increase so that you will know the answers even before you cast your runes. Every time it happens, keep track of everything that pops into your head regarding the reading, then check later if they confirm any of your earlier thoughts.

Now, on to the actual consecration process. Just like cleansing, there is no one method of consecrating runes. If you follow the basic requirements, then you will be fine.

First, you will need purifying smoke. Most heathenry practitioners use sage as its smoke has purifying qualities. Some people do not like sage as the smell of its smoke can be overpowering. If so for you, then you can use incense. For consecration, you cannot go wrong by choosing traditional frankincense and myrrh.

But if you are not a fan of fragrances, you can use a white candle instead. The warm light given off by the candle can also serve as a catalyst. You can choose whatever method works best for you.

Here are the basic steps for the basic consecration ceremony:

- Light the bundle of sage/incense and allow the smoke to flow over you and purify yourself and the container of your runes.

- Hold your runes using the non-dominant hand. Hold it over the sage/incense smoke or over the flame of the white candle. It should be just high enough over it that you feel no pain.

- Seek your deity's aid for protection and protect your runes from all, save for the highest forms of energy.

- Look at each run and connect with them one by one. Imagine your energy going into each and becoming one with it. Now, with your non-dominant hand, hold them all again and place them over the smoke.

Ask your chosen deity to consecrate them so you can use them to help yourself and others.

After cleansing and consecrating your set, you can use it immediately. When not in use, store them in a soft pouch or a lined box so they remain sacred and safe.

Chapter 6: Aettir: The Mother, the Warrior, and the King

According to many academic and occult books that focus on runes, the Elder Futhark consists of three aettir (aett for its singular form). Aettir's existence did not get a lot of attention even after the runes regained their fame, though, since the Enochian alphabet lacks its similar division.

The only things that form part of the Enochian alphabet's internal structure are numerology and alphabetic order. You can also see these two divisions in the Hebrew alphabet with an additional division between single, mother, and double letters. The only time when the use of aettir was mentioned was when they served as the basis of ciphers, like tents and twig runes.

Despite that, it is still important to understand aettir as it relates to the Norse magic and rune creation. The reason is that it plays a huge role, serving as the basis for numerology in runes, which is already a complex subject on its own. It serves as a system with a few implications regarding the use of runes. Aside from implying an initiatory structure, the aettir also reflects the ancient Aryan tribal society's division consisting of the nurturer (mother), the warrior, and the king (priest).

The Three Divisions

As mentioned earlier, the Aettir structures the runes in a way they have three divisions. Each division or group, called an Aett, has exactly eight runes. Each aett has the name of a God matching the group's or family's runes. Aside from that, all the Aettir concealed specific teachings individually. Also, you will notice each rune composing a similar aett to be connected with each other.

Frey - The Mother

Frey is the first group or family, which symbolizes fertility. It is the reason it is also classified as the Mother. It serves as the vital force together with the way it is demonstrated inside the human body. It is also about awakening your consciousness. As the first Aett, the Frey signifies the first few steps you have to take for your enlightened future. This means it is something you should track to reach your ultimate goal.

Heimdall - The Warrior

The God, Heimdall, leads this second division. He is viewed as the God of silence sometimes, which others also perceive as priestly meditation. In essence, though, Heimdall can be considered a warrior. He is a watchful warrior, capable of facing struggles and dealing with overwhelming odds. It is in his watchfulness wherein he shows endless courage.

Tyr - The King

This group, which can also be viewed as the King, shows people's relationship with the divine forces. It also encompasses the roles they play in fate. This aett also refers to the human condition. It symbolizes social aspects and men and women's spiritual transformation.

You will get to know more about these three divisions (Aettir) in this book's succeeding chapters.

What Does the Elder Futhark Runes Represent?

The three mentioned divisions come with their own set of runes (8 for each aett, specifically). Each aett that forms part of each division has complementary functions. Each also boasts of its own unique character. A total of 24 elder Futhark runes, each one has these characters:

- Symbol portrayed by the rune and what it means
- Rune's exact name – This also signifies the word's meaning and its value in the form of a letter.
- Energy composing the rune – This also encompasses the specific reason why those who practice the rune view it as a living symbol.

The energy connected to each rune is not still and static. It is in motion all the time. It changes and even evolves into other forms. By tradition, the Norse made use of runes to convey information from one generation to another. With that, it is no longer surprising to see these runes informing anyone interested in the cosmos legend and how the energies existed.

By understanding all these energies on a deeper level, you also get to understand the specific reasons they affect your life and how. Also, remember that each rune represents the whole of each cosmic energy that composes all the aettir. With that, it is possible for you to view these energies as treasure maps – those capable of showing you a clear path you can follow to achieve divinity.

Once you gain a full understanding of the runes and the manner through which you can use them, it will indicate that you are following Odin's footsteps. You follow his quest and hunger for knowledge as he seems to continue searching for wisdom even after becoming a god.

Contradictions in Runes

When trying to gather information about all the runes to master them, you will most likely realize that each rune comes with polarities. For instance, Fehu and Uruz, the first two runes composing Frey, the first aett, are classic examples there are contradictions. The reason is that while Fehu symbolizes fire, Uruz is a symbol of ice.

You can also expect to see the same contradictions within just one rune. Fehu, for example, signifies mobile wealth, knowledge, great riches, and the capacity to succeed in a lot of things. Fehu also feeds your jealousy, greed, and inability to achieve your personal goals now and then.

With these contradictions around, it is crucial to gain a full comprehension of the specific manner through which the polarities work. This is important, especially if your goal is to make the runes work favorably for you despite the contradictions you detected. With your knowledge and understanding, you can take full advantage of the runes, especially for enriching your life and that of others.

What to Expect from the Three Aettir?

Basically, the first aett is a symbol of creation. The second one is all about the human element, while the third one is all about achieving divinity. It is at this exact point where you can expect to see the energies getting unified. The good thing about each aettir is that it aims to end favorably. Among those that you can expect from each aettir in the end ae:

- Wunjo, ushering practitioners to the Golden Age
- Sowilo, which signifies the sun
- Othala, symbolizing the leap you have taken from a regular plane to the next level. This will prompt the start of the circular process again.

Do you remember the time when Odin was nearly at death while he was still hanging from the branches of Yggdrasil? It was also the time when he pushed himself deliberately to move from one rune and aett to the next. This was the move he took to acquire all sacred knowledge and wisdom in each one.

It is also important to know all aetts have individual sections, outlining and tackling every bit of information related to each rune. This section informs you about the numerous methods you can use to take full advantage of each rune, especially in achieving your goals.

Here, you will discover limitless energy patterns that can greatly influence your personality and your present activities, and your future, especially if you stick to your present path. Note that each of your actions has waves of energy. Each action develops ripples and stimulates certain reactions and responses that help in balancing them.

Generally, maintaining the right balance between each rune's contradictions is important. Like Odin's past actions, it is possible for you to go back to the divine, the specific aspect where you came from once you work with the energies of the runes and comprehend their wisdom completely. It is what will help you fulfill the runes' circle.

After completing one aett, you will be led to a new one with a higher level of understanding, and this cycle will continue endlessly. There is never an end in the quest for more knowledge. There is always room for new experiences and new levels of understanding.

If you think that you already understood Othala, which is the last letter of the Futhark, then you can study what Fehu can do for your daily life. It means that a new cycle of learning has begun.

The three aetts represent the stages in a journey wherein you, the traveler, need to deal with the mundane and the spiritual, best the obstacles that come your way, learn how to read and understand important information, and take time to rest and refocus before you start once again. Such is the way of the runes.

Chapter 7: Freya's Aett

This chapter will teach you all about the first aett of the Futhark, which is Freya's aett. For each rune, you will get an explanation on how to pronounce them, their meaning, how to interpret them during divination, and other pertinent information.

When learning the runic alphabet, remember that every rune can have multiple meanings. You will need to use your intuition to figure out which meaning fits into your rune reading circumstances. You need to know all the meanings, so you can recall them easily whenever you are doing a reading for yourself or someone else.

The first of the three Aettir belongs to Freya, who is the Norse goddess of love, beauty, and fertility. This aett handles all aspects of love, happiness, pleasure, physical presence, and human emotions. Freya's aett is also symbolic of new beginnings, creation, and growth.

Here are the first eight runes included in Freya's Aett to start you learning how to read the runes.

Fehu

Sound: "f"

Meaning: Cattle, Wealth, Gold

Fehu is the rune that symbolizes new beginnings and the start of a new journey. It also became the first letter in the Futhark. Fehu's definition of cattle symbolizes wealth and material possessions. If you have cattle, then it means you are wealthy. Material wealth also includes money in all its forms. It is not just about physically owning the currency.

Because Fehu is the first of the letters in the runic alphabet, it also represents new and fresh beginnings. Another meaning you can derive from the Fehu rune is good luck, strength, and hope.

This rune also symbolizes the Cosmic Fire streaming towards the Cosmic Ice. With that, it is no longer surprising why it can help you set things in motion. Fehu symbolizes the ring of fire you need to go through to discover new things or seek mysteries.

The thing about new beginnings is that they can be quite scary. Usually, such beginnings will require you to jump blindly into unknown territory. There, you can use Fehu to help you take that all-important first step.

In the later runic poems, Fehu is said to connect with the mystery of wealth. Remember that just using this rune or any other will not make you rich automatically. In the poems, the Fehu rune says that you need to circulate your wealth and your skills. You also have to deal them out freely to attract more wealth your way. Simply put, you need to give wealth to gain it.

To use the rune Fehu, you can work them into sigils for good luck, wealth, and abundance. It is also useful in spells that aim to reach similar goals. You can inscribe the symbol of Fehu in an amulet to encourage wealth and strength to come to you.

Uruz

Sound: "oo" (letter "u")

Meaning: Auroch, an extinct species of Northern European wild cattle

Uruz mainly symbolizes strength and vitality. Like the wild oxen this rune represents, Uruz will impart strength (physical and mental) and vitality upon the caster.

You can look at Uruz as the wild and more primal counterpart of Fehu, symbolized by domesticated oxen. When they roamed the European plains, the Aurochs were among the fastest and strongest of all the beasts in the land. It represents brute strength and primal power that allows it to resist getting tamed. Uruz is also symbolic of freedom. Aside from that, it is the creative force that drives new beginnings.

Uruz represents man's primal instinct and power. It also symbolizes the success you can only receive through hard work. Uruz is symbolic of the clash between two opposing forces of Fire and Ice. You can use this rune to transfigure living things and impart healing energy. It can also promote faster and more effective healing to those who are ill. Aside from that, you can use it on any task or situation that requires any form of strength.

The shape of this rune came from the horns of the majestic and strong aurochs. In legends and real life, the oxen are mighty, and sometimes, they are even holy. Oxen and cows provide sustenance. In some myths, they also helped in creating the cosmos. It is the reason aurochs, and in connection with Uruz, can be associated with raw strength and vitality.

If you place the rune Uruz on objects, you can use it to bolster defensive magic. Many people hang a horseshoe over the front door of houses for protection and good luck. The main reason behind it is that it looks like the rune Uruz.

You can use the rune Uruz during those times when you find the need to bolster or increase your strength. One scenario is getting into new endeavors or whenever you need to increase your creativity.

Thurisaz

Sound: "th" (corresponds to the sound rather than the letters)

Meaning/s: This rune represents the god, Thor, as he is the protector of the Aesir. It can also represent the giants and their resilience.

Heathenry practitioners believe this rune is symbolic of the human will and resistance against physical and mental assault. With that in mind, Thurisaz became one of the most popular runes among those who practice heathenry.

According to experts, Thurisaz's definition is about passive defense or protection against danger and negative energies. Think of how thorns protect the rose bush. The rose bush need not do anything to prevent animals and people from getting too close. The thorns will provide more than enough protection.

Thurisaz can also mean transformation or the process of discarding what no longer works for you so you can make room for other positive things that may come your way. It is a symbol of abrupt changes or scenarios wherein you need to make an important choice.

Thurisaz is Thor's rune, which is why it represents force and will. The energy of this rune is a reactive force. It symbolizes the way of pure action and impenetrable will. It is the action that one plans for, which is like an impulsive shield that goes up instantly to protect your mind from attacks. You can use it to protect yourself against mental invasions, including dangerous curses.

Thurisaz is also purported to represent the poisoned needle that supposedly placed Sleeping Beauty under an eternal sleep. You can use Thurisaz to cause sleep or otherwise awaken someone from a mystical slumber.

As you can probably tell by now, you can inscribe this rune into sigils and amulets that provide protection. Aside from protection, you can consult it for guidance when making important and somewhat life-changing decisions.

Ansuz

Sound: "ah" (a)

Meaning: This rune symbolizes the divine, specifically the Aesir and other deities.

Practitioners of heathenry believe that Ansuz is the rune of the mind and awareness. It is also called the rune of Odin. It represents everything about communication and wisdom. Aside from that, it symbolizes basically anything that concerns words. Whether you are seeking advice, heeding help in studying for upcoming tests (particularly verbal ones), and connecting with your inner voice, you will discover that they all, and probably more, fall under the rune Ansuz.

If you are looking into strengthening other runes, Ansuz is the one you need. You can also use it to limit runes' powers. It is also the one associated with tools used for thought and memory.

This rune has a connection with inspiration and, by association, with the arts. It is the reason you can usually find the rune inscribed on or watermarked onto sketchbooks, desks, parchments, quills, and anything related to writing and drawing.

Regarding the manner through which you can use this rune, one scenario is when you need help with communicating with others. You will also find it useful in effective decision-making and in ensuring that you can easily make divination.

Raido

Sound: "r"

Meaning: Raido represents the journey of a ride, particularly a cart. It is also called the rune of order and correctness.

Raido symbolizes any kind of journey, travel in general, or even a means of transportation/vehicle. The type of journey does not matter. Whether you are physically transporting yourself from one place to another or trying to experience a spiritual or emotional journey, the rune Raido symbolizes them all.

Consulting this rune will show you the different options you can take to reach your destinations. You can also consult it when you need advice on what you need to do to accomplish the goals you set for yourself. Aside from that, this rune can signify your need to decide on something important and otherwise.

Raido also represents good counsel, one that will lead you to the right path. You can find this right path when you think rationally, consider your situation, and weigh your possible courses of action depending on both reason and your tradition. With that, many members of royalty and elected public officials would often wear clothes inscribed with this rune.

Heathenry practitioners also use Raido in rituals to ensure there will be no mistakes made during the event. You may also want to inscribe the rune on the floor where you will often do your readings as it will minimize, if not eliminate, your chances of making mistakes.

Moreover, Raido is valuable for maintaining your rhythm. If you are a musician or a performer where rhythm is imperative, this rune can help you keep up with the beat.

You can incorporate it on amulets or a charm to protect you during your journeys. It can help you make important decisions that will let you move your life in the right direction.

Kenaz

Sound: "k"

Meaning: Kenaz represents the torch, more specifically, the light that emanates from it.

When you feel troubled because you believe that nothing is going right and you want to change the course of your fate, Kenaz can help you by illuminating the path ahead of you. With its illumination, you can see where you need to go. According to practitioners, Kenaz is the rune responsible for all aspects and forms of creativity.

Every time a good idea pops into your head, it is like a light bulb is turned on just to clear your mind of everything. Kenaz is responsible for that sudden burst of inspiration you just had. The reason is this rune is all about clarity, enlightenment, discovery, and knowledge.

You can also connect this rune to the element of fire as it can illuminate the path in front of you. In addition, it can destroy the obstacles on your path or clear the way so you will see even more options to take on your journey.

Kenaz is like a torch that will lead you toward unlocking your creativity and self-knowledge. The light from this rune allows you to focus on your personal work. It encourages you to become your own individual to stand out from the rest of the crowd.

The light of Kenaz can cause you to experience a sort of awakening within yourself, thus resulting in personal growth. This rune will help you know how to create something from nature or inspired by it.

For instance, you can carve this symbol into the trunk of a tree. It will force the tree to grow into the shape of the rune caster's liking. It can also provide you with a stronger wood for whatever use you plan for it.

If you are an artist, you can apply this rune to all your creations. For instance, if you are a painter, preparing a base coat with the rune Kenaz painted into it will help guide your brush strokes. That way, they will follow what it is you intend to convey in your painting.

If you are cooking, stirring the pot in the Kenaz shape can help you think of that one unusual ingredient that will give your dish the perfect taste. Creating amulets inscribed with Kenaz will also help attract external forces to increase your strength, power, and creativity to higher levels. You can also use this rune whenever you want to improve your insight, letting you come up with brilliant ideas for your creations.

Gebo

Sound: "g"

Meaning: The rune Gebo symbolizes the gift of the process of giving to others. It represents the relationship between the giver and the receiver.

Gebo is the rune of hospitality, giving, and, most especially, of sacrifice. Although Gebo is the symbol for a gift, it is not about the item itself. It is more on the meeting point between the person giving it and the one who will be receiving it. Gebo speaks to partnerships between individuals. It also talks about honor, commitment, and hospitality.

Gebo influences you to sacrifice for your fellow men whenever they need help. It helps you become more capable of following through on your promises. It prevents you from backing down from your words, regardless of whether it is to a friend or refers to a business transaction. But you can also use Gebo to make others sacrifice for your sake, but know that it will often backfire on you.

Aside from that, this rune can symbolize the force of the exchange of vows between two people, like in a marriage. The exchange of gifts between the wedded couple brings joy to both participants. This joy increases exponentially when the gifts have the Gebo inscription within them. This rune will increase the chances of a successful union filled with health and trust between the two.

Charms and runes inscribed with the rune Gebo effectively attract and encourage the propagation of harmony between people.

Wunjo

Sound: "v" or "w"

Meaning: The last rune of Freya's aett, Wunjo, symbolizes joy and bliss. It encourages happiness and contentment within people.

With that symbolism, not surprisingly, why Wunjo is also said to be the rune of harmony, joy, and holistic healing. Casting this rune indicates luck and success in your endeavors. It also represents personal happiness and having friendly relationships with others. If you are going through rough times in your life, casting this rune during your readings is a good sign that good things are bound to happen.

Because Wunjo is connected to happiness and bliss, it makes it a useful rune when used in items such as gift wrappers or the gifts themselves. You can also use it when cooking for yourself and others. Just stir the pot using the shape of the rune, and it will imbue your dish with its influence.

If you are to manage a group of people or your household's head, the rune Wunjo can help you with your task. This is evident by the number of organized groups, like sports teams, schools, and clubs that use the rune to decorate their door frames, wall décor, etc.

When dealing with a group of people with varying ideologies and beliefs, it will take a lot of work to keep them in harmony. Using the power of Wunjo will make this seemingly difficult task more bearable. Another famous use of this rune is as a decoration to hang over your front door frame. The symbol of Wunjo will help you attract happiness and success into your household.

Chapter 8: Heimdall's Aett

Heimdall is the watchman of the gods. His task includes guarding the entrance to Asgard, which is the rainbow bridge, Bifrost. Heimdall is an ever-watchful warrior, and even though he is the sole guardian of Asgard against invaders, he does not waver. As a matter of fact, he shows unending courage. He has keen ears and eyes, patiently waiting for the time when he can blow his horn and signal the start of Ragnarok, which is the end of the world.

The second aett in the Futhark is Heimdall's aett, and it deals with the concepts of conflict and making changes. The first rune of this set, Hagalaz, is associated with Heimdall.

Hagalaz

ᚺ

Sound: "h"

This is the first letter in Heimdall's aett. Aside from being the rune symbol for the said god, it is also that of hail or hailstones, which also means destruction. This rune represents how our need or want of something can put a restriction on us. It restricts our possibilities but also contains the power we need to break free from those restrictions.

Hagalaz is one of the few runes that are almost entirely about destruction. It is also the rune for hail because it brings forth severe damage and natural destruction. However, not all types of destruction are inherently evil or negative. Sometimes, you will need to take down the old and non-useful ones to make way for the new.

For instance, storms or blizzards must blow away the dead branches of a tree so new growth can appear in their place. In addition, the dead limbs and leaves will serve as fertilizers for the tree and the other plants surrounding it, so they will grow taller.

If you get the Hagalaz run from a reading, then that means you should let go of the things from your past that may be hindering you from progressing further. It is like excessive nostalgia, which prevents you from making changes to things you are used to, even if you will greatly benefit from its results. One great way to use this rune is to make it part of a ward against natural disasters or bad weather.

Naudhiz

Sound: "n"

Naudhiz is the rune for necessity. It could be material gifts or anything intangible. Some also call this the rune of urgency, denoting that change is necessary, and everyone will need it soon. This rune's key concept is that it is nearing the time when you have to balance things in your life. You have to cleanse yourself and harmonize with the universe once more.

Naudhiz is the representation of how people's own needs and wants to serve as limiting factors to their growth. However, they also serve as the power that the same people need to use to break free from their restraints. It is all about how you use it.

This rune signifies the need to cut out the things in your life that hold you back and keep you from growing as a person. When you get this rune during a reading, it is crucial to reach deep within and ask yourself about the specific things you think you have to let go of.

Naudhiz also means using your unbiased thinking when making huge decisions in life. It may require you to let go of your personal biases and look at the situation from a bird's eye view so you can make a good decision. It is the best rune to use when divining for the perfect mate or partner. Moreover, it is ideal for spiritual and physical transformation that will lead to the perfect balance.

Isa

Sound: "i," "ee"

As the rune of ice, Isa denotes the standstill that blinds or impedes people from moving forward. These are the psychological stumbling blocks that prevent you from thinking or acting. It is telling you to turn inwards and examine the meaning of yourself.

Another meaning you can derive from the Isa rune is conflict resolution, denoting the need for mending relationships and/or clearing misunderstandings to move forward in life. You can also interpret Isa as conservation and self-preservation. It states you should look inside yourself to discover what you are doing that could limit your growth. It is saying you should help yourself first before you can do so for others.

Because Isa denotes conservation, it is good to use this symbol on your canned food or any other stocks you stowed away for later. The rune will help impede their aging processes, thereby giving them a longer shelf life. You can also carve this rune on the doors of your cupboards to attract similar energy.

Jera

Sound: pronounced like the "y" in "year"

Jera refers to the rune of harvest. It is also the rune that denotes the cycle of life. The key concept includes abundance. Just like when the harvest season arrives, every household has an abundance of food.

Jera represents the passage of time. It is the symbol of the cycle of the seasons and how it repeats all the time without fail. With the completion of one cycle comes growth, the fruition of the plans you have set into motion, progress, and your growth as a person.

However, Jera also has some negative aspects. For instance, this means you should expect retribution for any bad deeds you have done in the past. The reason is that everything always comes back full circle. It also symbolizes the repetition of negative behavior you should eliminate as soon as you can.

If you get Jera in your reading, then note it also means you will be seeing the results of your earlier efforts. It may be telling you you will be getting that promotion you have been working hard toward or finally paying off your loans.

If you are using the rune, you can carve it on the fence posts of your garden. By doing that, you will be blessed by bountiful harvests and protect your plants from disease and drought.

Eihwaz

Sound: "eo" "ae"

This rune symbolizes the yew tree. It is also called the rune of endurance. Just like the yew tree, you can expect it to be more enduring the longer it stands. It can affect matters that require the use of consistent strength.

You can read Eihwaz as a quality of peak endurance that will not waver even when facing adversity. You can also read it as dependability. It is like someone who will be ready to help you even at his own expense.

Eihwaz also indicates that you are enduring enough; you are viewing obstacles in your path as steppingstones to reach your goal. You know how to fail upward. You are also patient enough to know how important it is to wait for the right time to make your move. This means you do not make hasty judgments.

However, there is a negative side to using this rune – that is, you may face a lot of confusion. The reason is that you will not understand what you should do next. It could also mean dissatisfaction, which can prevent you from feeling happy with the results of your tasks.

Because Eihwaz is the rune of endurance, it is best to carve this symbol onto the handles of tools you plan to use for many years to come. You can also turn it into an accessory to wear during rune crafting. It can help ensure that the ones you make will pass the test of time.

Perthro

Sound: "p"

The rune, Perthro, symbolizes the Dice Cup. It represents a dice cup tipped on its side, spilling the dice contained within and releasing the luck (or lack thereof) contained within.

It is also called the rune of gambling and taking risks. It is also more commonly known as the rune of mystery. It basically encompasses everything that is unknown in man's realm and the excitement of taking the plunge into a new endeavor.

It is also the rune that represents many secrets. Perthro is symbolic of the uncertainties and mysteries in life. It also symbolizes a mortal man's free will and the restrictions that come with it.

This rune has negative effects, though. Among these negative effects are delusions of grandeur, failure of risks taken, and generally all powers beyond man's control. This rune can also lead to overindulgence in gambling and delusions of winning the next hand every time.

To use Perthro outside of divination, you can stitch it into the gambler's wallet or purse. You can also put it in your logo if you are starting a new business. You can take advantage of the influence of Perthro in anything that deals with taking risks or trying new things.

Algiz /Elhaz

Sound: "zz"

Also known as the rune of protection, Algiz represents the Elk. It has a three-pronged design, which symbolizes the antlers of the stag. This rune represents the sudden urge of wanting to protect oneself or others from danger. It also means warding off evil and misfortune.

It has great restraining power, high defense, and protection. If you come up with it during your casting session, then you might need protection soon. Maybe someone you know can benefit from your protection.

Another definition you can read from Algiz is communication coming from the spiritual realm. It is like someone close to you who has been gone for some time is trying to talk to you or send you a sign.

If you get a reversed reading of Algiz, then it is highly likely there is danger lurking in the dark, or a sinister force is driving you away from the protection you are seeking. It may also indicate that someone will be turning his back on anyone who needs help. It is unknown which side you will be on.

In the olden days, warriors would carve the rune Algiz onto their shields for protection. In these modern times, though, when using swords and shields are out of fashion, you can just get a tattoo of the rune on your shield arm. It is your non-dominant arm, and it will provide you with the same form of protection.

Sowulo/Sowilu

Sound: "s"

It is the last rune in Heimdall's aett, which represents the sun. Many practitioners also call this the rune of power. Unfortunately, it was also the source of the Nazi's infamous Swastika symbol. This rune's definition can be extended to include clarity of thought, power, masculinity, and victory.

If you are seeking the help of this rune, you are asking for the ability to see with utmost clarity. It would be like the sun shining its light into the darkness to expose all that was once hiding in the shadows. This rune can also offer you guidance whenever you are figuratively in the dark with no idea what action you need to take to move forward.

Other readings you can glean from the Sowulo rune are good health, optimism, and confidence, among many other positive things. Basically, if you can come up with this rune during your rune casting sessions, you can somehow expect good things to come.

However, when you come up with the reverse of Sowilu, you can expect negative things like sudden, unexpected changes that can alter all your carefully laid out plans. It may also put you at risk of experiencing false success, not reaching the goal you set out to reach or gaining bad counsel you will most likely follow, unfortunately.

Historically, the Sowulo rune would be inscribed on stones that glorify the fallen soldiers. You can also use it as a sign to glorify Thor. You can inscribe this rune onto an amulet whenever you need additional courage to face adversity.

Chapter 9: Tyr's Aett

The god, Tyr, represents protection and complete victory. He is also the symbol of cosmic justice and all the things that relate to the politics of rulership. This aett concerns itself with intellect, spiritual growth, and understanding without judgment.

If you get a majority of the runes belonging to Tyr's aett during a casting session, then it could indicate that you are too inactive in achieving your goals. It could be you are overthinking your moves, or you are not centered because you are still uncertain of what you want.

Tir/Teiwaz

Sound: "t"

The first rune in Tyr's aett is coincidentally named after the god itself or at least a version of his name. It represents victory and justice, just like the deity. It is also called the Creator's rune.

Just like Sowilo, casting Tir usually promises success in your endeavor, but it may require you to make a personal sacrifice. Whether you will make a sacrifice or not will be the catalyst for your success. This rune also works well when embroiled in sticky legal matters, but only if you are in the right.

Just like the beginning of Heimdall's aett, Tyr's aett begins with a loss. However, it is a sacrifice you will do voluntarily. Unlike the hail sent down by the gods, the loss you will experience at the beginning of the third aett is under your control. You can get through without the sacrifice indicated, but this will be difficult.

However, to gain the benefits from the succeeding runes, make that sacrifice. Just like when Tyr had to sacrifice one of his hands so Fenrir, the gigantic and powerful wolf that was said to bring forth Ragnarok, could be shackled.

When you get a reversed casting of Tir, the consequences include loss of self-confidence, becoming an untrustworthy person in the eyes of your peers, and cowardice. In other words, you become the type of person who is weak, not just physically but mentally, and emotionally.

As mentioned earlier, this rune may help you sway the judge's favor toward your side, so carve its symbol on a small piece of wood. It should be small enough to fit in your pocket. You should then bring it with you to the courthouse.

Berkano/Berhano

Sound: "b"

This rune represents the Birch Tree. It represents a new beginning, like a birch coming to life from a similar tree from a seed buried in the soil. Berkano represents fertility and of having a home in complete peace and harmony. If you are planning to have a new member of your family, you can strive to gain the blessing of this rune.

It is also the perfect rune when trying to deal with concealment and secrecy. If you have something private and you wish to keep it that way, you may find the power of Berkano useful. The reason is that it ensures that you or anyone else will be spreading your secret around for everyone to see.

The Berkano is primarily oriented towards the feminine. However, you will notice it looks like a pair of breasts. It is a nurturing rune as indicative of it being oriented towards femininity. You can expect healing in both the physical and spiritual manner.

When cast in the negative, Berkano can cause secrecy within all household members, immaturity, and lust instead of fertility. In the worst-case scenario, a reversed Berkano may also signify abandonment.

To use this rune, you can carve it into a bedpost of a couple trying to conceive. You will also find it useful when placed in barnyard stalls where livestock are expected to bear their young.

Ehwaz

Sound: "e" as it sounds in "every"

Ehwaz represents the twin gods, the Alcis. You can often picture it as two brothers on horseback and linked by a wooden beam. This beam symbolizes the strong partnership between the twin brothers. It means that one cannot move without the cooperation of the other.

The rune Ehwaz is the Norse symbol for the horse, which represents partnership. As such, it deals with anything that concerns partnerships, like marriage, relationships, and business relations. Appealing to this rune will strengthen the bonds between the partners.

Casting this rune also means a new journey. For instance, you may be due for a job change soon or discover that you will need to move to a new home because of a job transfer. Just like the rune Tir, Ehwaz signifies a new start, but it may involve giving up something in return.

Another meaning you can divine when you cast Ehwaz is following the natural flow of a task you have in hand. It means learning how to work well with others instead of constantly butting heads. It also indicates learning how to depend on others, making it possible for you to accomplish all your tasks.

This rune's reversal may denote a couple of negative things, like treachery and reckless haste in doing tasks, which often ends in disaster. It could also mean breaking up standing partnerships.

In neo-pagan unions, the couple would paint the rune Ehwaz on their hands as a symbol of their everlasting partnership. They also do so as proof of trust and loyalty toward each other. And you can carve this rune on a plaque and hang it above your headboard.

Mannaz

Sound: "m"

It is the rune that symbolizes humankind. It can either represent your race or just you, the individual. This rune is incredibly special. You can apply it to situations and purposes that serve a social nature. It also helps strengthen bonds between the members of a group and develop a rational mind to deal with squabbles.

Casting Mannaz means undergoing self-analysis and inward reflection. If you find yourself stuck on a task and cannot seem to figure out what you need to do to advance, you can cast it hoping to find the answers to your questions.

Mannaz may also indicate the need to work on your personal reputation and people skills. Casting Mannaz when you have trouble working with other people may represent your desire to improve yourself instead of trying to find fault in the other members of your group. On the other hand, it can also mean you and your team have a strong bond with each other, and there is nothing you can't do when you work together.

Now, when Mannaz is in the negative, it may mean there will be a small problem that gets blown way out of proportion, negatively affecting your partnership. There are also instances when it signifies that you are unwittingly sabotaging your relationship and that your bond is getting weaker by the day.

You will do well to inscribe this symbol on your dinner table as that is where you and your family usually discuss family matters. It will amplify the bond you and your family share, leading to productive discussions.

Laguz

ᛚ

Sound: "l"

This rune represents the element of water and its flowing nature. It symbolizes the sheer power of water as well as its ability to follow the path of least resistance when it is flowing. Laguz is also symbolic of human thought and how you need to use it for good.

When you get Laguz from your rune casting, one way to read it is a safe harbor or place that offers you sanctuary from all the negativity in the world. Alternatively, it may not even be a place. It may symbolize a supportive partner or harmonious relationship you can count on when troubled.

Drawing a Laguz also indicates you were right to follow your intuition regarding any of your tasks at hand. Just like the flow of water, you let your intuition guide you toward the right path. You did not need to overthink and come up with your own obstacles. Laguz means you should let your unconscious mind take over occasionally as it may come up with a better idea.

A Laguz positioned in reversal, on the other hand, may indicate that you are emotionally manipulated, either by someone else who is close to you or even yourself. It could happen when you come up with excuses not to do something that is supposed to benefit you in the long run.

Carving this rune into an amulet or anything similar can aid in the further advancement of your mental abilities. It means you can learn even more. Another benefit of having a Laguz effect is that it can further enhance your intuition, making you much better at making decisions.

Inguz/Ing

Sound: "ng" as in the word "long"

Inguz is the Rune of Sexuality, which means it has power over physical attraction toward others, and ultimately, sex. This rune affects sex, but Inguz is only mostly concerned with the act in terms of reproduction and fertility.

Casting Inguz also means having the ability to spread your energy as far as you want to. It makes it possible for you to influence more people or provide more individuals with protection. However, to use the power of Inguz properly, it is important to build up your energy over time. Once you reach a certain level, you release it all at once.

During a reading, getting Inguz may also indicate the need to use more of your common-sense during decision-making if you tend to follow suit with what everyone else around you is doing without considering what could happen to you. Seeing this rune can help you figure out if you have to step back and use your common sense to realize that you are on the wrong path.

There is nothing much to worry about if you get a reversed Inguz rune during your casting, as it usually deals with minor inconveniences such as lust and immaturity. However, it may also signify decreased libido or infertility.

You can use Inguz in many ways aside from rune casting. For instance, you can carve the symbol on a piece of wood that is small enough to keep in your pocket. It will increase your chances of attracting a mate. You can also carve this rune on your bedpost to improve your sex life.

Dagaz

Sound: "d"

Dagaz, also known as the Rune of Transformation, represents a huge transformation, which might be of the spiritual, mental, or social type. Also called the Rune of Daybreak, it signifies the change between night and day, which is vast, to say the least. If you are seeking guidance when you need to make an important decision, Dagaz is one of the runes that can help.

Casting Dagaz also denotes the need to reconsider your current circumstance and whether you need to make a drastic change. It means you are questioning whether your decision is correct or not.

Another meaning you can get from Dagaz during a casting session is stability between opposing forces, such as light and darkness. You are getting hints on whether you need to certainly adjust to attain balance in your life.

The good thing about this rune is that it rarely has reverse effects. However, if the Dagaz rune gets surrounded by opposing, reversed runes, it could mean you have to look forward. You may also have to stop dwelling on the past too much.

Because Dagaz is the Rune of Transformation, it would work well when inscribed on the doors of a school or any other learning institution. Better yet, you should be able to find it in rehabilitation centers because those who are checked-in want to transform into much better versions of themselves.

Othala/Othila

Sound: "o" like in "old"

Othala is the Rune of Loyalty, which represents fealty to one's family, clan, tribe, country, or even cause/belief. Like Fehu, Othala is symbolic of wealth. However, unlike Fehu, Othala's wealth is intangible. This wealth is family, culture, heritage, and friendships. Othala represents a kind of enclosure and a way of maintaining the status quo.

Getting this rune during a reading usually connotes issues regarding your ancestry birthright. For instance, there may be something big going on in your hometown you would do well to at least inquire about.

This rune may also signify something related to your immediate family. For instance, a sibling of yours may want to reconnect after many years of not speaking. Another meaning might be that you will be called upon by your country or culture to lend your skills, like enlisting in the military. You may also work toward protecting your heritage soon.

Now, the most obvious negative effect of this rune is developing racism, bigotry, and general xenophobia. One unfortunate instance of the use of this rune was during World War II when Othala was engraved in the knives issued to the Hitler Youth members. Should you want to use this rune to gain its energy, you have to do so aided by something connected to family matters, like a family crest.

Memorizing the Futhark Runes

Now that you have learned about the three Aettir and the runes within them, you may be somewhat overwhelmed at how unfamiliar they are to you. It is understandable since you are essentially trying to learn a new alphabet.

However, there are mnemonic devices you can use to make it easier to implant the Futhark runes into your memory. One of the best and easiest ways to do so is to associate the symbol with their basic meanings.

First, let's tackle the first eight runes of Freya's Aett.

- **Fehu** – This rune means cattle, which connotes movable wealth. It has two lines jutting out from a vertical line, pretty much like the horns of a cow. Also, this rune looks like the letter "F," which it represents.

- **Uruz** – This means auroch, an extinct wild ox used to live in parts of Europe. Uruz represents primal power, and it looks like an upside-down "U." It is roughly the same as the profile of a bison or any other large land mammal.

- **Thurisaz** – This means thorn or thurs (giant), and it represents danger. It does look like a thorn. Imagine a stem with a single thorn jutting out the side. It also represents the "th" sound.

- **Ansuz** – This means as (a god), specifically Odin. It also represents Odin's domain, which is communication. This rune kind of looks like the letter "A." To remember it with ease, just associate it with the word answer. Coincidentally, Ansuz also represents the letter "A."

- **Raido** – This is the rune associated with travel. It may mean to ride a vehicle to get to your destination. Moreover, it looks like the letter "R," which it also represents.
- **Kenaz** – This rune means torch, which is a symbol of illumination and knowledge. Imagine a beam of light coming from a flashlight, starting from a small point and then radiating outward. This rune also looks like the letter "C," and it represents the sound of "c" or "k."
- **Gebo** – This means gift and has connotations pertaining to relationships and hospitality. It looks like the letter "X" and similar to the ribbon on a present.
- **Wunjo** – This rune means joy, and it looks like a pennant flag, the kind you would wave when your favorite sports team is winning the game. Speaking of winning, it also starts with the letter "w," which this rune represents.

These are the first eight letters of the Futhark. To remember the order of the runes, recite, "the Futhark is a gift of joy." The first six spell out futhark, while gift and joy are the meanings of the last two (gebo and wunjo).

Now, let us move onto the runes in Heimdall's Aett.

- **Hagalaz** – This rune means hail or hailstones. It represents huge changes or crises, much like the destruction left behind by a huge hailstorm. It looks like and represents the letter "H," which is the first letter in hail.
- **Nauthiz** – This means need, and it looks like how a person would rub two sticks together if he needs fire. It represents the letter "N" and has negative connotations for being needy.
- **Isa** – This means ice, and it represents stasis wherein everything is still, just like everything around you when it is winter. It looks just like an icicle and represents the letter "I."

- **Jera** – This rune means year (the "J" is pronounced like "Y"), and it symbolizes a year's harvest, something that you need to work for. This rune resembles two cupped hands ready to receive their hard-earned reward. It represents the letters "J" and "Y."

- **Eihwaz** – This rune represents the yew tree. Often, it also signifies the Yggdrasil itself. It symbolizes the mysteries of life and death. You can imagine the shape of the rune-like a sparse tree with one branch and one root. It also represents the sound "ei" (pronounced "eye"), which you can easily link to Odin, the one-eyed, who hung from the branches of Yggdrasil for nine days.

- **Perthro** – This means dice cup and symbolizes gambling and divination – two of the things where you can use a dice cup for. It is shaped like a dice cup tipped over. The name of the rune contains the sound throw, which is what you do with dice.

- **Algiz** – This means elk and the rune. With its three prongs, it looks like the antlers of a deer. The shape indicates a trident, which you can use for defense and keep enemies at bay. Remember the last letter of this rune's name because it also symbolizes the letter "Z."

- **Sowilo** – This rune means sun, and it represents energy and victory. Sowilo sounds like solar. It also looks like the letter "S," which it represents.

We have come to the end of Heimdall's aett. To remember the sequence of the runes, you can use the sentences "Hail needs ice harvesters. I was destined to protect the sun."

The first sentence consists of the meanings and associations of the first four runes. In the second sentence, "I was" sounds like eihwaz, and the rest of the sentence corresponds to each respective runes' associations.

Let's conclude with Tyr's aett. Here they are:

- **Tir/Tiwaz** - This rune's name is one version of Tyr's name. It represents honor. It resembles an arrow pointing upward, specifically towards the sky, and Tyr is a sky god.
- **Berkano** - This means birch goddess, and it is a rune of blessings and fertility. It resembles the letter "B" and represents it, too. Blessing starts with the letter "B," and so does the word baby.
- **Ehwaz** - This rune means horse, and it does look like the side profile of a horse, one with a saddle in the middle. When turned on its side, it looks almost like the letter "E," which it represents.
- **Mannaz** - This means mankind, and it is the rune of social order and awareness. It also looks like two persons with their arms locked in unity. It also resembles the letter "M," which is one thing it represents.
- **Laguz** - This means water, and the rune looks like the sail of a ship. The name laguz sounds like the word lagoon, which is a body of water. It also looks like an upside-down letter "L," which it represents.
- **Ingwaz** - This represents the god Ing (Frey), and it means seed. This rune symbolizes fertility, agriculture, and growth. It looks like vines that intertwine with each other while growing. The name of the rune has the "ng" sound, which is what it symbolizes.
- **Dagaz** - This means day, and it essentially means awakening or awareness. It also appears like the emergency alarm speakers, the kind that wakes you up and makes you jump into action. It also looks like two "D's" standing back-to-back.

- **Othala** - This rune means home, belonging, or inheritance. It resembles the roof of a house. Since it starts with the letter "O," it also represents that letter.

Now that you have memorized the eight runes of Tyr's Aett, here is a mnemonic device you can use to remember their order: "Tyr blesses horses and men; sail-ing all day back home."

Chapter 10: Odin's Rune

Aside from the usual 24 runes that compose the Futhark runic alphabet, modern neo-pagans and heathenry practitioners have introduced an extra blank tile in their rune sets and gave it the name Wyrd, which means fate.

Total emptiness or infinite possibilities? Depending on how you look at it, there are many ways through which you can read Odin's rune. This rune was a later addition by modern neo-pagans to get some additional chance from the cosmos when casting runes. Users of this rune say that when Odin's rune appears in your cast, it means that the unknown is at work and it is there even if you cannot see it.

Even though many rune casters use Odin's rune these days, its actual meaning is still hotly debated. Some say it means endless possibilities, while others say it indicates emptiness. It is like the glass half-full or half-empty conundrum.

What Does the Blank Rune Mean?

Whenever you get a blank rune, take note it could signify that you ran into some complications with your casting. It may be a hint that your inquiry is not worded properly, or it may be that the answer you are seeking is impossible to grasp (or maybe deep inside, you already know the answer). Take it as a sign you need to meditate and wait for before giving your reading another shot.

The consensus about Odin's rune is there is none. If you ask ten people about it, you will also get ten answers. There is no one definition of the blank rune. Any potential user can use it on whatever day they want to.

In his book "A Handbook for the Use of an Ancient Oracle" (1983), Ralph Blum said that the appearance of the blank rune is an omen of death. However, that death might just be symbolic and not an actual passing of a person. It can also refer to a certain part of your life gone and replaced by another.

According to Lisa Peschel, author of "A Practical Guide to the Runes: Their Uses in Divination and Magick," whenever this rune appears, the only thing you can expect is that something unexpected will happen to you. This something can be positive or negative depending on whether you have been virtuous. It is also best to interpret its meaning by basing it on how it relates to its neighbors.

Kylie Holmes, the author of "Pagan Portals: Runes" (2013), said that casting the blank rune indicates there is progress in your spiritual development. This act also reminds you how large your knowledge is. It is bigger compared to how other people view it.

In over a millennium of its existence, there have been very few modifications to the runic alphabet. These variations are usually geographic, and the shapes of certain runes were the only notable changes. Their meanings remained the same. However, there has been a modern addition to the Elder and Younger Futhark runic alphabet, and it is the Wyrd rune.

There has been no solid evidence that the Wyrd (also called Odin's rune) existed before the resurgence of using runes, and its origins are muddy, to say the least, but even so, it is included in most rune sets these days.

What Makes the Wyrd Rune Different from the Rest?

The Wyrd rune is often just a blank tile in the set, but some say it looks like this:

This rune symbol represents all the rune shapes molded into one. According to old beliefs, it is possible to make this rune by yourself aided by clay or any similar material. Regardless of your chosen material, it would be necessary for you to get a tiny pinch of material from the other runes to produce a new and blank one. It is the blank rune that serves as the culmination of all other runes' powers.

The blank rune differs from the others in the sense it does not belong in the three Aettir of the Elder Futhark. It is only a modern addition that originated around 40 years ago in the 1980s when the New Age revolution was just taking over Western culture. However, even though it is a new addition to the runic alphabet, most modern rune casters still widely accept it.

The blank rune is also distinguishable from the rest of the runic alphabet because it is mainly a part of an ancient alphabet. This means that except for Wyrd, every rune represents a sound or combination of sounds. Some practitioners say that Wyrd represents silence, making it a unique concept since you can find no alphabet in the world with a symbol for silence.

Traditional beliefs also indicate that blank runes existed for the sole reason of having a replacement tile if a loss occurs or misplacement of another tile. Purists also believe that the blank rune does not fit into the runes' mathematical and mystical system. The reason is that you can't merely divide 25 tiles into four (four seasons in a year, four cardinal directions, and others).

The Wyrd rune does not have its own set of definitions. You can even view it as total emptiness or infinite possibilities. Some also view it as a sign of unseen forces moving in the background to affect your fate.

Why is it Called Odin's Rune?

Another name for the Wyrd rune is Odin's rune, as it has unfathomable and mysterious power and meaning. Odin is the All-Father, the ruler of all the gods of Asgard, and yet he did not stop his quest for more knowledge. You can associate the blank rune with Odin, not only because of his omnipotence but also due to his constant hunger for more knowledge.

When Odin appears before you during a reading, he is calling out to you to look deep within yourself to achieve a deeper, more profound understanding of yourself and your being. The blank rune represents the human's almost unlimited potential, and it will be up to the reader how to take this knowledge.

It is also one reason Odin's rune does not belong in the Aettir. Odin stands alone, separate from the other aesir. Bringing any further meaning to Odin's rune would be like trying to tie a string around all the Nine Worlds. It would be futile and impossible.

How Should You Read the Blank Rune?

Although not all rune casters believe that the blank rune should be included in any rune sets, there is nothing that prevents you from using it if you want to. If you want to use Odin's rune in your readings, here are a couple of suggestions on how you can read it.

The early Anglo-Saxons, and many of the other tribal races hailing from present Northern Europe, believed in the universal force called Orlog, which means both "doom" and "destiny." Orlog oversees the fates of all the nations and their citizens. One way to read the blank rune is to base it on the concept of Orlog. This means that your individual fate is bestowed upon you by the Norns if you pull this rune.

The blank rune might mean you have karmic debt, and the cosmos is collecting payment. Now, your karmic debt might not be due to your past personal actions but from your past life. This may seem like it is unfair that you are responsible for what you did in your past life, but then again, it will also be the case for your next life. With that in mind, drawing the blank rune may mean you need to do better in your present life.

Another possible definition of the blank rune may be that you have reached a certain point in your life where you have reached the point of no return. You are destined to a singular fate soon, and you do nothing to change it. Even though you still have free will, it will not matter whatever you do now. The results will still be the same.

Now, if you pull out the blank rune in response to a specific question, it means it is not the right time for your query. It is like a Magic 8-ball telling you you should try asking again later. The cosmic fates may still cook something up for that part of your fate, so it will not register in the runes just yet.

Another definition you can get from the blank rune is that you will be experiencing huge changes in your life. However, because of the ambiguous nature of the blank rune, you cannot be sure if the change will be positive or negative. It could be getting a huge promotion and raise at work or losing a family member. You need to be careful if you seem to get a huge change in your life.

Should You Use the Wyrd Rune?

It totally depends on you if you want to keep the blank rune in your rune set. Purists might scoff at you behind your back if you use this rune. Some may even find it blasphemous that you even think of using a rune that was not a part of the Elder Futhark. However, using the blank rune will provide you with one that represents nothingness and how it can affect your life.

Also, remember that not everyone is as accepting of the blank rune, especially the purists, who see it as a sacrilegious abomination. They view the blank rune as an unwelcome product of the New Age lightheadedness and the ravenous appetite for sacred symbols. For them, a rune is a symbol, not an absence of it. A symbol for the absence of a symbol is not a concept used by the Norse. It is an oxymoron, and it contradicts itself.

However, despite many people rejecting the concept of the blank rune, it will be going nowhere soon. It is an idea ingrained in neo-paganism for 40 years. Through all that time, it has been enduring continuous scrutiny and dismissals from the community. It has become such a fixture it compels rune makers who choose not to add it to their sets for sale to mention it on their labeling. It happened even though the original set of 24 runes did not have it, and it was only introduced in the 1980s.

The question remains, should you use the blank rune? The final answer will always depend on you. If you want your rune readings to be as close to the ancient traditional rune reading, then avoid using the blank tile. If you are open to possibilities and are like many of the New Age neo-pagans, then there is nothing wrong with using the blank rune in your set. You can try using it when doing readings on yourself to discover if it fits into your reading style.

Now that you know what it is, how it came to be, and how to use it, you can form your own opinion about it. Whether you use it or not, it will not change that it is already in the mainstream rune reading scene and may continue to do so for quite a long time.

Chapter 11: Reading the Runes

Rune layouts and spreads can help you make sense of what they are trying to tell you. While each rune already has its own inherent meanings, you will need to know when those interpretations will come into play in your life. Using layouts and spreads will provide you with a structure designed to promote ease in translating the message of the runes.

What is the difference between layouts and spreads? You can't really find that many! If you are familiar with using tarot cards, you will discover that rune layouts are like tarot card spreads. Several rune casters use tarot card spreads when doing readings. In this sense, you can use layout and spread interchangeably.

Choosing which layout or spread to use is not that difficult. If you have only a simple question, you can use the layouts that use the least number of runes. If you have a complicated problem you need counsel for, a rune layout that uses more runes is in order. The more complex the problem, the more elaborate the spread.

Rune Casting Layouts

Here are some of the most commonly used layouts for casting runes:

One Rune Layout

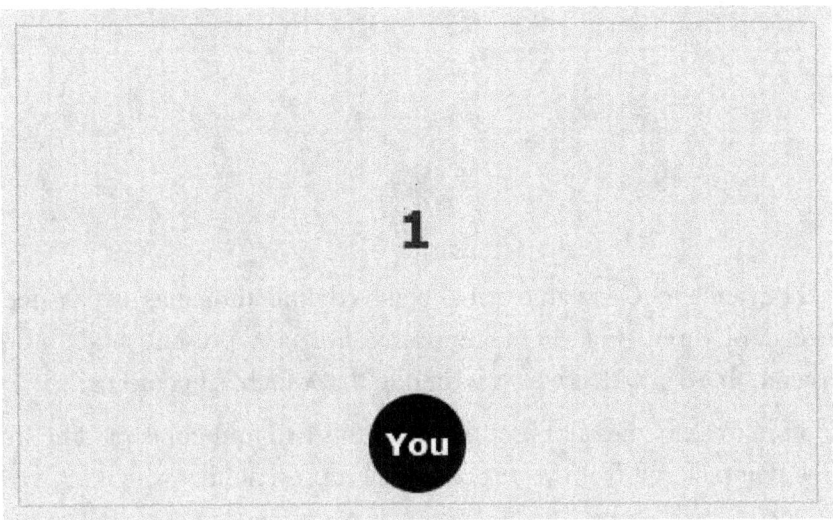

It is the most basic out of all the rune layouts as it only requires a single tile to read. You can either cast a handful of runes onto your rune cloth or pick the one that seems to call out to you. It is a great way to do a quick reading to help you with a sudden decision.

You do not even need to use a casting fabric nor remove your hand from your pocket. If you can read the rune by touch, you can get your answer in just a couple of seconds. It is possible to read this rune as your general feeling and attitude you feel toward the question. It also represents the outcome you will receive from the question.

Two Rune Layout

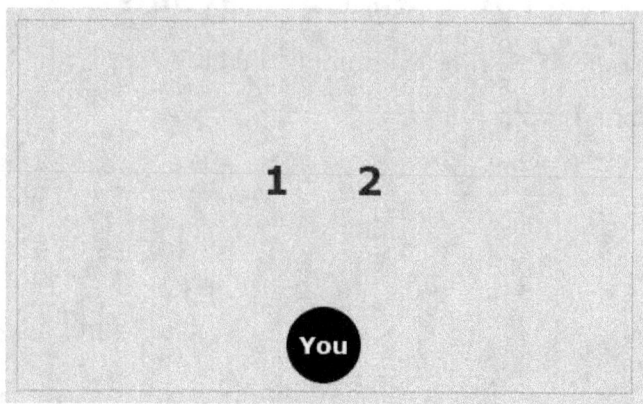

The ancient Germanic tribe believed that time has two aspects instead of three. For them, there are no past, present, and future. Instead, there is a "that which is" and a "that which is becoming."

The two-rune layout based itself on this two-fold concept. The first rune you pick out from your pouch will represent "that which is," while the second will symbolize "that which is becoming."

The first rune (that which is) includes the things that happened in the past and how it can affect the question asked. It will make you think back on your past actions. Did you really do something to warrant the cosmos to put you into the situation you are in?

The second rune (that which is becoming) encompasses the ways through which the events of the future, and the future, can affect the question asked of the runes. You might not be able to prevent any bad situations from happening. However, you can at least try to react differently to your reading.

Three Rune Layout (Past, Present, and Future)

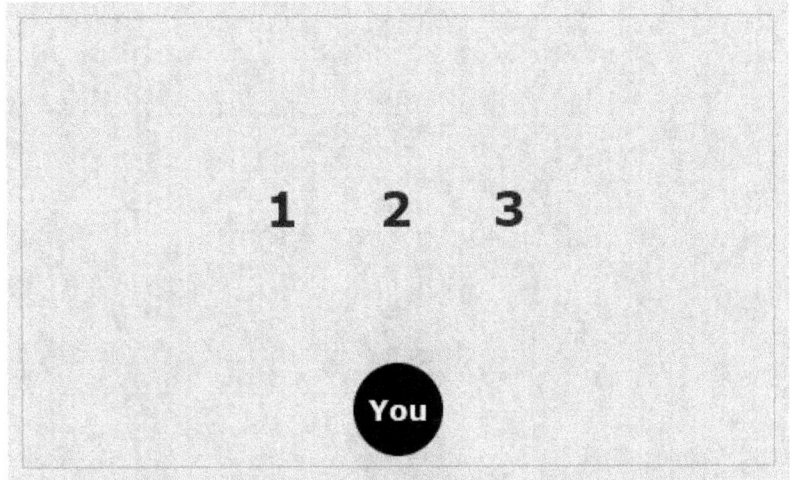

Not everyone agrees with the old Norse two-fold concept of time. You can use the three-rune layout to take advantage of the three-fold concept instead. The rune on the left, which is most likely the first one you cast, represents the past. But the middle is the present, while the one on the right is the future.

The past includes the events with a significant effect regarding the question. They are like the actions you did in the past that may be why you are in your situation.

The present refers to the things happening that affect your situation regarding the query. The future is just simply the outcome of the question you asked.

Unarguably, the three-rune spread did not exist during the ancient times when the Norse were still around. However, if this configuration speaks to you, no one can hold it against you if you want to use it.

Four Directions Layout

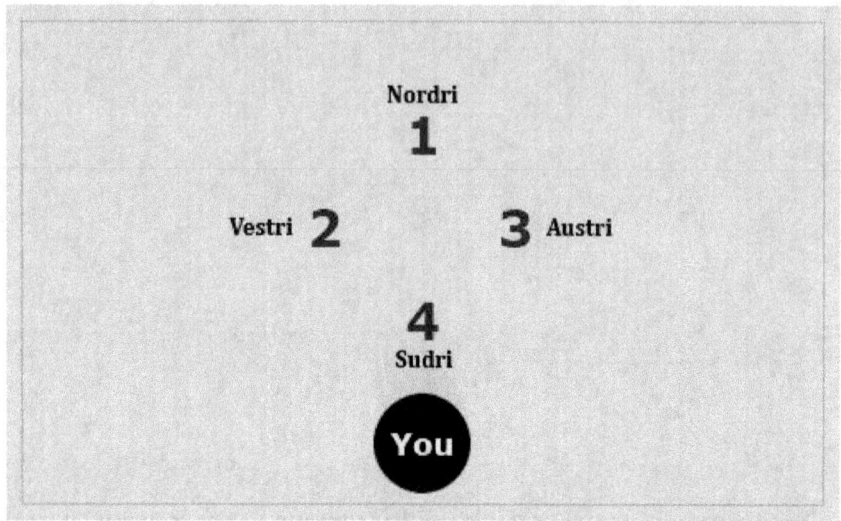

Because the runes came from Norse mythology, the four cardinal directions' names are named after the four dwarves that legends say are holding up the sky. It is made of the skull of the giant Ymir. The concept of this layout is simple. It is just a normal North, East, South, and West pattern with different meanings for each position, namely:

- **Nordri** – This represents the past, particularly influences that have effects on the past regarding your question.

- **Vestri** – This is the present, namely the things currently happening with an effect on the question that you asked.

- **Austri** – This represents the future and the possible obstacles you will encounter that might hinder the outcome of your tasks.

- **Sudri** – This is the total possible outcome of the reading.

There are things you need to know regarding this casting choice. First, it is like the three-rune layout because the past, present, and future are all involved. However, it is not the Austri rune that will predict the future for you. Sudri will take on the role played by the usual future position, instead.

Five-Rune Cross Layout

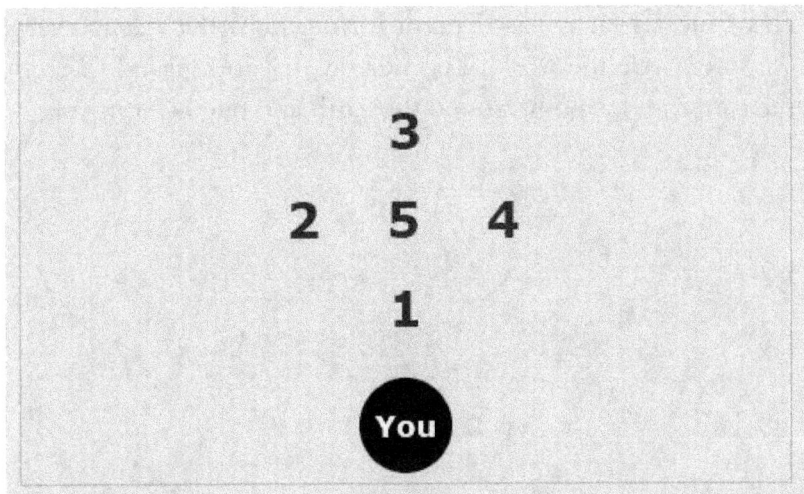

With this reading layout, you will be forming a cross shape with the five runes you have to cast on the cloth. The first will be at the bottom of the cross; the second will be at the left position, the third on top, and the last one will be at the center of the cross.

- 1 - It represents the general things that might be underlying in the question.
- 2 - These are the obstacles you will need to overcome to get your answer.
- 3 - It represents the beneficial processes you might experience.
- 4 - It represents the possible outcome/s.
- 5 - It will show the future influences that could affect the outcome.

Midgard Serpent Layout

This rune layout is based upon Jormugandr, the gigantic serpent known to encircle the world. Legends say that Jormugandr is so huge that he can wrap his body around the earth and bite his own tail.

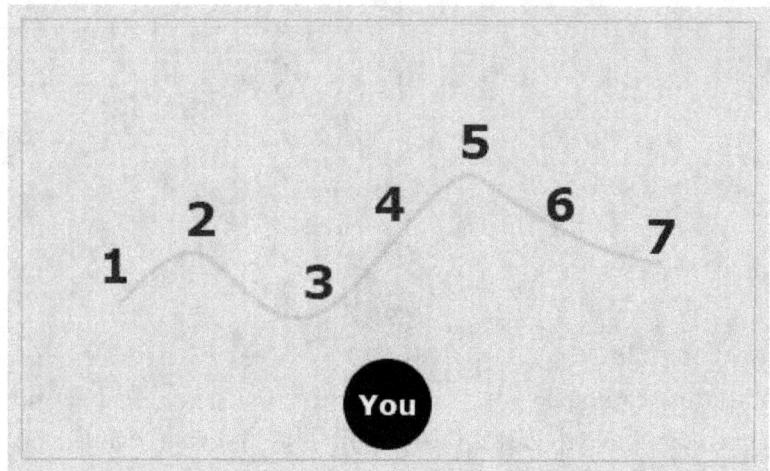

This is symbolic of how you need to be completely aware during the reading, or else the results of the layout might pass you by.

You will be setting up the seven-runes in a flowing pattern and imagine walking from the tail of the Midgard serpent up to its head. There will be a couple of uphill sections where you will be experiencing obstacles. However, note there will also be downhill sections where you can relax, making it possible for you to prepare yourself for the next uphill battle.

- 1 – It symbolizes your feelings in the past and their connection to the situation you are asking help for. Did you do something that resulted in your predicament?

- 2 – It represents the struggles that you have to go through because of your feelings from position 1. The hump represents the obstacles you overcame and that you need to know how you handled the past situation because it might come back to you in the present.

- 3 - This point represents your feelings about your situation. It is the rune nearest to your position because it roughly represents the present.

- 4 - It is the position where you start on your journey toward your desired outcome. The obstacles from the previous positions may come back to you. The hump at this position is also much steeper than the one at position 2, meaning the obstacles you need to face are more difficult than before. However, you now have the guidance from the past to help you.

- 5 - It is the peak of your journey where you can see your goal. This rune will show you your feelings and how they can control you when you think that your goal is within reach.

- 6 - It is the position that will remind you that there is still a bit more work to do before you reach your goal. You need to take heed of this rune the most. If it is telling you you need to put more effort, then do what it says. For instance, if you happen to cast a rune of power and control, you must be strong-willed and control your emotions until you reach your goals.

- 7 - It is the Midgard Serpent's head, and most of the time, it is the final goal. However, according to Norse mythology, Jormugandr could bite its own tail, so it is crucial to be mindful of what the runes are saying. Otherwise, you may find yourself back on the tail of the serpent.

Bifrost Layout

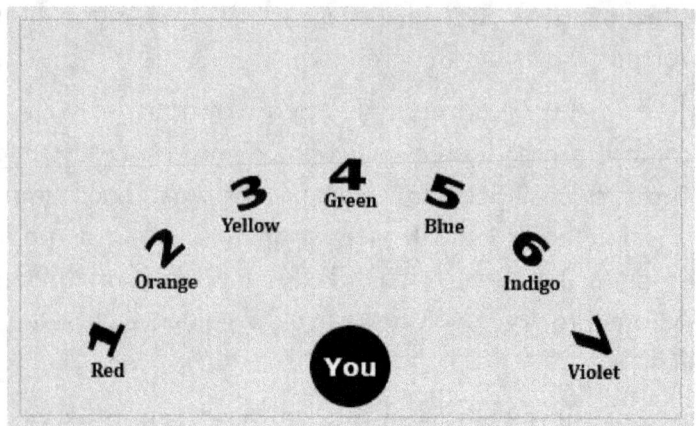

According to Norse legends, the Bifrost is the rainbow bridge that connects Midgard, the realm of humans, to Asgard, the realm of the gods. By using this layout, you will be getting a sense you are getting help and guidance from the gods themselves. You will be casting seven runes and place them in an arcing pattern, starting from the left to the right. At the start is the color red, and it will end with the color violet.

- **Red** – It encompasses your attitudes from the past that might have some effect on your inquiry.

- **Orange** – It represents the effects of the past that result from your past attitudes.

- **Yellow** – This rune represents your attitude at present with an effect on your question.

- **Green** – It represents the effects of your current attitude on the overall outcome.

- **Blue** – The rune represents what kind of attitude you need to have in the future.

- **Indigo** – It symbolizes the effects of the attitude in the future.

- **Violet** – It represents the overall outcome of your journey.

This layout might seem like a complicated one. However, if you examine it closely, it is still just a past, present, and future layout with a couple of exceptions.

Grid of Nine Layout

The Grid of Nine requires that you cast nine runes and lay them out in a grid, like the one below. Ensure that you follow the numbering shown, as it plays an important role in the reading effectiveness.

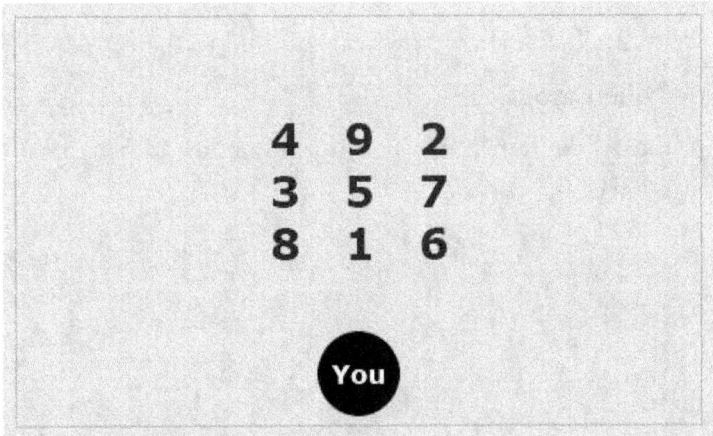

The special thing about this grid is that if you add the values of any row or column, even the diagonals, you will always end up with an answer of 15. To read this layout, begin with the lowest horizontal row first. This row represents the factors from the past that influenced the matter at hand.

- 8 – It refers to the hidden influences that happened.
- 1 – It encompasses the basic influences you experienced.
- 6 – It represents your current attitude towards the events from the past.

You should then follow it up by reading the middle row from left to right, including:

- 3 – These are the hidden influences that are acting at present.
- 5 – It will represent the current status quo.
- 7 – It refers to your attitude toward the things happening in the present.

Last, you have to read the top row as it represents the outcome of your inquiry. It consists of:

- 4 – This refers to the hidden influences, the obstacles that prevent the outcome from surfacing.
- 9 – It is the absolute best outcome of your question.
- 2 – It will show how you respond to the result.

Odin's Nine Layout

Odin, the All-Father, hung from the branches of Yggdrasil to gain the knowledge of the runes.

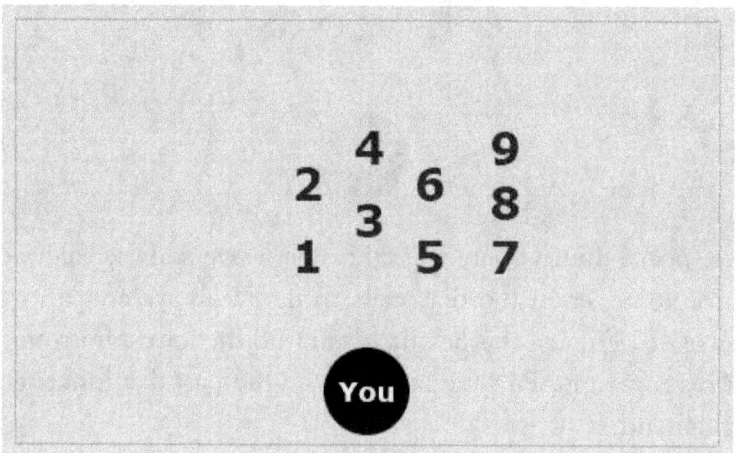

The first six runes represent Odin himself (1 and 2 are the legs, 4 is the head), and the last three are for Odin's spear. To read this layout, follow this:

The runes in the first column (1 and 2) represent the factors in the past that might have influenced your question.

- 1 - It symbolizes the hidden images that happened in the past.
- 2 - It is your attitude toward the past.

The column with the runes 3 and 4 represents the current affecting the outlet.

- 3 - It encompasses the hidden influences currently happening.
- 4 - It is the questioner's attitude regarding current events.

The column with the runes 5 and 6 will tell you about the answer to the question.

- 5 - This rune represents the hidden influences. It also symbolizes the causes of delay that may prevent the answer from manifesting.
- 6 - It is your response to the answer.

The last column (7, 8, and 9) represent the powers you either have or have to deal with. These figures represent the powers you have to take care of for the first, second, and third columns, respectively.

Celtic Cross Spread

Although this spread is usually used for tarot card reading, you can also use it for rune reading. You will need to cast ten runes from your pouch then lay them out in the same pattern as you would when reading tarot cards.

Before you cast, though, concentrate on the particular rune you would like help from. For instance, if you are trying to conceive, get a rune that represents fertility. Concentrate on getting it as you cast the ten tiles needed for this layout.

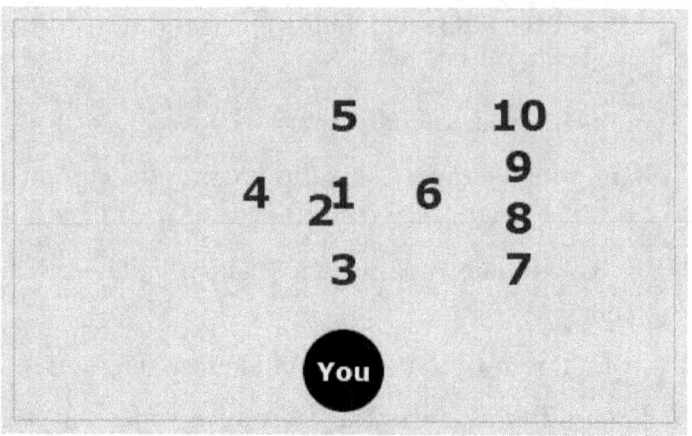

If possible, place rune number 2 over number 1. To gain understanding from this rune spread, here is how to read it:

- 1 - This represents the question at hand.
- 2 - It signifies the forces that might oppose your question.
- 3 - It covers the underlying influence that may affect the answer to your question.
- 4 - It shows the influences you are passing through or ending.
- 5 - It encompasses the influences that might become important in the long term.
- 6 - It represents the many influences you may come across soon.
- 7 - It refers to the fears and negative thoughts you may have.
- 8 - It points to the outside influences that can potentially influence the outcome.
- 9 - It refers to your beliefs and hopes.
- 10 - It will provide the best outcome for your inquiry.

This layout may seem a bit complicated, so to make it easier, imagine Odin standing in front of you with his spear held by his left hand.

Egil's Whalebone Layout

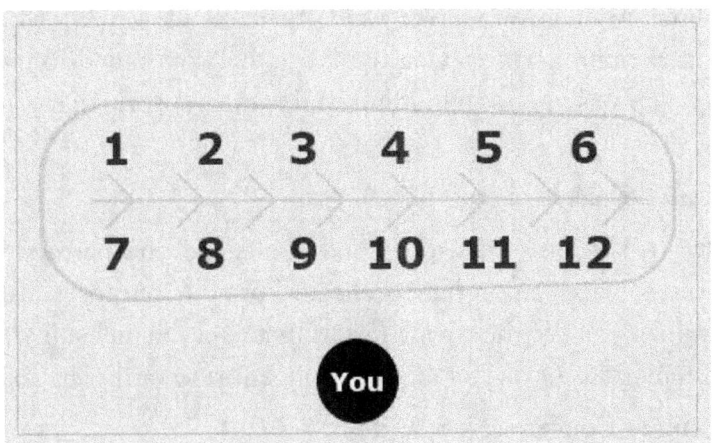

This rune layout took inspiration from the Icelandic saga "Egil's Saga," which is about a master poet, warrior, and runemaster, and his many accomplishments. There is a chapter in the saga wherein Egil cured Thorfinn's daughter Helga from an incurable disease. The reason Helga was sick in the first place included the wrong runes placed on her head. Egil removed the erring runes and replaced them with the new ones he carved into whalebone, instantly curing her.

For this layout, you will be doing something that differs somewhat from the other readings. Instead of each rune having a different meaning, you can group them by threes and read as if the group is speaking. It is basically a three-rune spread but doing them four times in one layout.

The four groups of runes derived their names from their purpose in the saga. Now, you do not have to read the entire saga before you can use this layout, but it can help. Knowing the story can help you remember what each group stands for.

Carver's Intentions (1, 2, and 3)

In the story, the rune carver had specific intentions for the runes. The first group acts just like that. You have a certain intention you want to consult the runes for. Before you cast the first three, think hard about what answers you want them to show you. Keep this intention in mind while picking out those that you intend to use. You need to keep this intention in mind while you are working towards the answer.

Helga's Results (4, 5, and 6)

Helga is Thorfinn's daughter, and she is the one harmed by the errant runes placed upon her forehead. For your purposes, this rune group will let you see the wrong results that could manifest if you have impure intentions or do not intend to put effort toward your goal.

Thorfinn's Concerns (7, 8, and 9)

Thorfinn is Helga's father, and in the saga, he worries about his daughter as she lays sick and dying on her bed. This group of runes is symbolic of the external concerns on your way to your goal. They can either be helpful or disruptive.

These outside influences can serve as support and help you on your way toward your intended goal. For instance, if your end intention is to become financially stable, these outside influences may come in the form of family and friends who help you when you are down in the dumps or help you find a more stable and higher-paying job.

The outside forces can also have a negative effect and may even hinder you from reaching your intended results. Using the example earlier of becoming financially stable, the outside forces may be your family or friends with ridiculous spending habits. They are influencing you to make irresponsible spending.

This group of runes will show you the things you need to keep an eye out for. Such could be helpful or destructive, and it will be up to you to discern which is which.

Egil's Results (10, 11, and 12)

Egil is the runemaster in the story. When he saw the runes, the state that Helga was in, and Thorfinn's concern for his daughter, he still made everything right again. Through his masterful skills of manipulating runes, he undid the previous rune maker's damage and made Helga healthy again.

This does not mean you need to recast your runes until you reach your desired outcome. This last set of three runes will only teach you how you can overcome the things you previously learned to achieve your goal. It also does not mean you can just disregard the previous three groups. It tells you how you can still reach your goal while remembering the possible difficulties that came from the first three groups. Think of the first three rune groups as a heads-up as to what you can expect on your journey so you can prepare yourself for the challenges.

The neat thing about rune layouts is that you have a choice whether to stick with the traditional ones (the one, two, three, or four rune layout) or make up your own. If you do the latter, make sure that it at least makes sense to you. The most important thing is that you use your insight to decipher what the runes are telling you based on the circumstances of the person asking the questions and the possible definitions, as stated by the runes themselves.

Chapter 12: The Poem of the Gods

Rune poems list down the letters of the runic alphabet and provide poem stanzas that explain each one's meanings. These poems were presumably made to be mnemonic devices designed to make memorizing them easily.

Three surviving ancient rune poems go back to the Middle Ages. The Icelandic and Norway rune poems were based on the Younger Futhark, while the Anglo-Saxon one is based on the Anglo-Saxon runes. Unfortunately, none using the Elder Futhark have ever been found yet.

Rune poems are more than just tools for memorizing the runes. You can also use them as chants to bolster the power inside each rune tile. It is also possible to use the poems to beckon and call upon the energies bound to each one, making your readings even more powerful than before.

Fehu

Wealth is won, and gold bestowed
But honor's due to all men owed
Gift the given and ware the lord
For thy name's worth noised abroad

In the older rune poems, one can see that money and its effect on relationships is vital. Money and wealth are important, but what you do with them is even more significant. Keeping money to yourself can lead to a reputation of being a miser. But grasping at what amount of money other people have will only lead to conflict.

Fehu is the rune of wealth, but it is also how you make and use it. It is about your community and how everyone shares whatever they can. It is about sharing your good fortune but also gracefully accepting help when you are in a bind.

Uruz

Wild ox-blood proud, sharp hornéd might
On moorland harsh midst sprite and wight
Unconquered will and fierce in form
Through summer's sun and winter's storm

Aurochs are wild oxen that once roamed the plains of Europe during the Middle Ages. It differs totally from the domesticated cattle mentioned in the previous rune Fehu.

In Runic terminology, Uruz symbolizes the unsurpassed will of explorers, the internal drive that allows you to set goals and achieve them. Without willpower, you become listless and insecure. It is the power you need to weather the storms that you are likely to encounter on your journey towards your goals.

In short, Uruz calls upon you to keep your focus and achieve the goals you set out for yourself. Also, it serves as a warning that there are multiple challenges on your path that will test your mettle.

Thurisaz

Thorn hedge bound the foe repelled
A giant's anger by Mjolnir felled
Thor protect us, fight for troth
In anger true as Odin's wrath

The thorn advises you to be cautious and aware of potential danger and challenges ahead. Unwittingly charge into thorns or grab a thorny vine, and you will pay for your lack of caution. If you fail to heed warnings, then you will pay for your actions.

You can also view thorns as protectors. For instance, keeping a hedge of blackthorn or hawthorn bushes will keep wild animals and certain human foes from invading your home.

Thurs, or giants, represent another kind of danger. These are often representative of the destructive and uncontrollable forces of nature. They can also be the forces within yourself that overwhelm you when you find yourself in a compromised position.

Ansuz

In mead divine and written word
In raven's call and whisper heard
Wisdom seek and wise-way act
In Mimir's well, see Odin's pact

Ansuz is the rune of wisdom. It is also the rune of listening to the voices that link you to the divine. Besides that, it represents being aware of the patterns of power and synchronicity around you. If you need increased wisdom or guidance or are just looking for the right words to say, invoke Ansuz.

Raido

By horse and wheel to travel far
Till journey's end a followed star
Harsh the road and sore the seat
Till journey's end and hearth-home meat

This rune represents traveling and the times when the journey comes with hard work, loneliness, and uncertainty of when it will end. Just like most journeys, they seem easy when planning for them. You will discover later that the road before you is full of obstacles and inevitable delays that will either make you want to turn back or power through them and grow.

Sometimes, the journey is about traveling and not the destination. The obstacles that block your way will also serve as challenges that will only make you stronger, but only if you do not give up.

Kenaz

Hearth and hallow, forging fire
Light the path and heart inspire
Torch of flame we hold on high
Guard the hall and burn the lie

Fire symbolizes dedication and transformation. It is also applying your truth, even if doing so comes at a personal cost. The same fire can also strengthen and empower you. It can provide focus and guidance. It is just like how a strong fire can temper and strengthen a sword.

Gebo

Lovers kiss and gift the hand
Lord's men shout and pledge to band
The gift is given back and thrice
In duty bound and honor's price

The gift-giver shows the receiver their appreciation. In return, the receiver is beholden to the giver, otherwise known as owing thanks. Gebo is the commitment between people. It is about trust, loyalty, and doing the right thing toward others. It is about putting your trust in other people and expecting them to do the same to you.

However, it does not mean that the receiver is technically the slave of the gift giver. There should be mutual respect coming from both sides. The receiver should give favor to the giver out of the goodness of his heart.

Wunjo

Harvest in and cattle fed

Table full and blessings said

Peace and joy in life be ours

With ease-full days and golden hours

This symbolizes the phrase, count your blessings. You need to focus on the good things you already have. They are gifts you need to enjoy wisely. Be thankful for the blessings you have and do not mind what you do not have.

Why would you fill your mind with negative thoughts when you can think of all the blessings you have received so far? You might even realize that you are at a better place in life than you first thought you were.

Hagalaz

Storm born hail as heaven's seed

Brings us pain and direst need

But ice corn melts in Solar's light

And waters crops in place of blight

Hagalaz can be read as a warning, but it can also serve as reassurance. Hailstorms do tend to be destructive, but thankfully, they are also quite short. And afterward, the hail will melt to water, which nourishes the earth. If some circumstances disrupt your plans, they often come with the seed for more benefits. More than anything, it is a lesson that will teach you to be more patient and accepting.

Nauthiz

This want constrains and binds the will

Yet drives us on to conquer still

Let need-fire burn when darkness falls

And summer seek when winter calls

Nauthiz symbolizes the fear of the unknown or what you would do if you found yourself where you feel trapped, and nothing seemed to go your way. This rune teaches courage in the face of adversity and creativity under pressure so you can keep searching for solutions rather than giving up.

Isa

Blue its beauty and smooth the way

But yet beware lest foot betray

As Niflheim's ice meets Muspel's fire

In Ginnungagap see Midgard spire

The rune Isa says go forward and take care but do not be full of fear. It also gives the promise there are good days still ahead. Winter may be cold and harsh, but it does not last forever, and it is not all gloom. If you take care and you know what you are doing, then the snow and ice hold a particular beauty.

It is like skating on a frozen lake. If you are careful and you take the necessary precautions, you will have a fantastic time. However, if you just jumped into the middle without taking care, you may just break through the ice and seriously hurt yourself.

Jera

Seasons turn, and sunsets follow
As seeds once sown are reaped the morrow
So harvest seek at summer's end
And till the soul for winter's mend

Jera is the rune of a certain kind of wisdom. It is the wisdom of growing old, letting go of some of your unattainable dreams, and embracing what will happen. Jera teaches people they should not fight their fate. What they should do, instead, is to go with the flow.

Jera teaches you not to fight against the current of life. It would be best for you just to relax and let yourself be carried by the flow. That way, you will reach your destination faster, and you will not be as spent as you would most likely become when you fight against the current.

Eihwaz

Yew bow drawn to guard the hearth
World tree spans a nine-fold path
From mystic tip where Eagle dwells
To Serpent roots, Yggdrasil's wells

Because yew trees have always been the tree of choice for graveyards and it is also poisonous, it has always been associated with death. However, that same poison is used by shamans to aid them whenever they want to travel to other worlds. It often leads them to answers they would not have access to otherwise.

It is not advisable for you to use poisonous yew to bring you closer to the gods as you may not be able to go back. Just invoke the Eihwaz and let it lead you towards enlightenment.

Perthro

From Urd's dark well is Orlog spun

Our past the path we have become

But life's womb still has choices yet

Until our doom and fate are set

Perthro is the mystery rune, meaning you cannot be entirely sure of what it represents. It is the rune of gambling, so the answer you will get will be uncertain. The cosmos have not decided on your fate, so you still have time to change it to however you want.

If you like to partake in some gambling (no judgment here, the ancient Norse like a bit of gambling as well), you can seek help from Perthro to guide your hand.

Algiz

Hands are lifted the Gods to praise

Blessings given to guide our ways

Protected be on ancient paths

Keep homelands whole, and safe our hearths

This is a rune that can help you when seeking divine intervention. However, you need to respect whatever hand is dealt to you and follow the path opened to you if you asked for it. You also need to invoke this rune if you wish protection upon yourself and upon your home and family.

Sowilo

Victorious shines the sky-shield wheel

By sailors watched to guide their keel

Shed healing rays and lift our souls

Give courage strong to win our goals

Sowilo, as a rune, is the one that challenges you, calling upon you to be courageous and as virtuous as you can be. Even though Sowilo is the rune of victory, you need to be actively participating in the battle if you wish to be part of the eventual victory. If you feel like nothing you are doing makes a difference in your life, implore the help of Sowilo to give you enlightenment and guidance on what you need to do.

Tir

A god's right hand for Fenrir's demand
Honour proved at the wolf's command
Tir defend us when all is lost
And teach us to give sacrificial cost

Tir is a constant reminder that even the gods will sometimes need to do the right thing to protect others, even if it meant that they need to sacrifice something in exchange. Tir is not just for justice for yourself. It also means you act just towards other people. It is doing the right thing even if you are not rewarded and even if it meant that you lose something.

Berkanaz

Birch mother goddess bringing hopes to birth
Show us our place and all nature's worth
Mystery enfolded and teacher of life
Keeper of doorways and Allfather's wife

Berkanaz is the rune of life cycles and the rune of the feminine and nurturing aspect. It will help show you your place in the natural order of things. Whenever you feel like you are lost and do not know where you belong, Berkanaz can help.

Ehwaz

Rider and ridden made one from the two
Both called together to work something new
Not earth bound but flying; spirit set free
So Odin rides Sleipnir along the world tree

The rider trusts his steed to carry him into danger and not buck him off its back, and the steed trusts its rider to protect it should the need arise. The rune Ehwaz is for close partnerships. It makes use of two energies combined to achieve something bigger than the sum of their parts. Ehwaz is about balance. It is about your skills and abilities taking precedence over your petty pride and selfishness.

Mannaz

To Ask and to Embla, to make humans whole
Ve, Vili, Odin, gifted blood, sense, and soul
Bound to the earth, yet filled with the other
We are joined in the life-boon, sister and brother

The rune Mannaz is about being human and how you use your gifts and honor them in everything you do. It also serves as a reminder that when you die, the gods can take your gifts away. It poses a challenge to the goals you set. Mannaz also calls upon you to become proud of your heritage as one being born of the gods.

Laguz

As leek grows from earth, bright green to behold
Wisdom and knowledge within will unfold
Water, the other world, spirit, and death
A doorway to pass through, beyond human breath

Laguz is the rune about water and anything connected to it. It could be a journey over a huge body of water, floods, and more. It is also about talking about your emotions, inner life, mind, and soul. It involves talking about your mental health.

Laguz also challenges you to contemplate death and the death of those around you, and not just the mortal body. Try to think about what happens to the soul when the mortal body perishes.

Ingwaz

Seed sown is rooted and nurtured for birth
New life beyond sight safe deep in the earth
Joy find in joining, sharing our pleasure
harvest and ploughing, each in true measure

The rune Ingwaz calls upon you to live your life as you wish and support others as they live theirs. This rune also celebrates the inherent potential in your life and everyone else's. You are your own person. You need not seek validation from others. You can live your life however you want to and treat others with the same respect you would expect from them.

Dagaz

To daylight from darkness, the circles return
Seeing the hidden, the wisdom we learn
Act now and surely, trusting thy heart
True flies the arrow, straight from the start

The symbol for Dagaz has two halves, which can possibly be interpreted as night and day. You can also call upon this rune if you need additional focus and the ability to concentrate totally and not get easily distracted by fear.

This poem speaks about the transition from night to day when the objects previously wrapped in shadows are becoming visible once more.

Othala

The greatest of treasures, more precious than gold
The gift to the young, passed from the old
As we tend to the roots, so the tree tip will flower
And sweet to the soul, the fruit of the bower

The rune Othala urges you never to forget your roots and where you came from. Also, you should never forget all the struggles you and your family had to go through so you could be in the position you are in right now. Othala challenges you to set aside your selfishness and always consider the greater community's needs before yours.

These poems are more than just simple mnemonic tools. All tell a story about the runes and their message. You will do well to memorize these verses and recite them whenever you are doing your readings. You will feel that you are closer to the divine. Besides that, your readings may even become more concise and accurate than they were before.

Conclusion

Now that you have reached the end of this book, you already know all the basic knowledge required to do your own rune readings. This knowledge should be enough for you to develop the ability to consult the runes yourself whenever you need some divine intervention or if you think you need advice on any aspect of your life.

Even though the ancient Norse is no longer with us in this world, their mystic arts are still present in these modern times. The art of rune reading is still alive and kicking today. Some might even say it is trendy. In fact, you will not find it hard to locate other like-minded people who share the same interest in runes as you do.

Here's another book by Mari Silva that you might like

Your Free Gift (only available for a limited time)

Thanks for getting this book! If you want to learn more about various spirituality topics, then join Mari Silva's community and get a free guided meditation MP3 for awakening your third eye. This guided meditation mp3 is designed to open and strengthen ones third eye so you can experience a higher state of consciousness. Simply visit the link below the image to get started.

https://spiritualityspot.com/meditation

References

Aettir, the three divisions of the runes- Aett. (n.d.). Tirage-Rune-Magie.net. Retrieved from http://tirage-rune-magie.net/us/rune/aett-aettir.htm

Aettir-The Three Divisions of the Runes & Their Use in Rune Magic. (n.d.). Www.Sunnyway.com. Retrieved from http://www.sunnyway.com/runes/aettir.html

Choosing a rune set: A beginner's guide. (n.d.). Grove and Grotto. Retrieved from https://www.groveandgrotto.com/blogs/articles/choosing-a-rune-set

Freyr's Aett (Archive) - Ancient Runes. (n.d.). Sites.Google.com. Retrieved from https://sites.google.com/site/mhancientrunes/textbook/section-1

HEIMDALL'S ÆTT - Marc Pugliese. (n.d.). Sites.Google.com. Retrieved from https://sites.google.com/site/marcapugliese/chapter-6/heimdall-s-aett-1

https://www.facebook.com/dattatreya.mandal?fref=ts. (2018, July 27). 12 Major Norse Gods And Goddesses You Should Know About. Realm of History. https://www.realmofhistory.com/2018/01/29/12-norse-gods-goddesses-facts/

Instructables. (2009, December 11). How-To Read Runes. Instructables; Instructables.

https://www.instructables.com/id/How-To-Read-Runes/

Norse Religion. (2015, July 3). Norse Religion. ReligionFacts. http://www.religionfacts.com/norse-religion

Scribes, J. S. (n.d.). RUNES - Care, Cleansing, Empowering and Storage. HubPages. Retrieved from https://discover.hubpages.com/religion-philosophy/RUNES-Care-Cleansing-Empowering-and-Storage

The Rune Site | Formerly Ankou's Page of Runes. (n.d.). Www.Therunesite.com. http://www.therunesite.com/

TYR'S ÆTT - Guido's Wyrd. (n.d.). Sites.Google.com. Retrieved from https://sites.google.com/site/themindofguido/chapter-6/tyr-s-aett-1

Variety Of Rune Spreads - Celtic Book of Shadows. (n.d.). Celticbookofshadows.Wikidot.com. Retrieved from http://celticbookofshadows.wikidot.com/variety-of-rune-spreads

Your Guide to Rune Divination. (2015, October 7). Rune Divination. https://runedivination.com/your-guide-to-rune-divination/

www.ingramcontent.com/pod-product-compliance
Lightning Source LLC
Chambersburg PA
CBHW062055280426
43673CB00073B/180